JESUS AS PRECURSOR

SOCIETY OF BIBLICAL LITERATURE

SEMEIA SUPPLEMENTS

Edited by

William A. Beardslee

Number 2

JESUS AS PRECURSOR

by

Robert W. Funk

JESUS AS PRECURSOR

by

Robert W. Funk

FORTRESS PRESS

Philadelphia, Pennsylvania
and

SCHOLARS PRESS

Missoula, Montana

PRINTED IN THE UNITED STATES OF AMERICA

1 2 3 4 5

Printing Department
University of Montana
Missoula, Montana 59801

1-1502

TABLE OF CONTENTS

JESUS AS PRECURSOR

Assistant Editor	Char Matejovsky
Design Consultant	Bruce Walter Barton
Composition	Linda Henry
Layout	Helen Melnis
Production	Diane C. Sharbono

Acknowledgments

Three of the essays in this volume were delivered, in a slightly different form, as the *Showers Lectures*, Indiana Central College, Indianapolis, Indiana, during February 1975. The three essays are: "Jesus as Precursor," "Jesus as Magician," and "Jesus as Saunterer." On that occasion President Gene E. Sease and Dr. Adolf Hansen were cordial hosts. I should like to thank them and the students and faculty of Indiana Central College for the opportunity to try these essays out before an appreciative audience.

"Jesus as Magician" was also delivered earlier at the School of Theology at Claremont as the Colwell lecture.

"Jesus and Kafka" appeared originally in the University of Montana *CAS Faculty Journal* (I, 1, Fall 1972: 25-32).

"The Parable of the Leaven" appeared in its original form in *Interpretation* (25 [1971] 149-70) under the title: "Beyond Criticism in Quest of Literacy: The Parable of the Leaven."

"The Looking-Glass Tree is for the Birds" appeared in *Interpretation* 27 (1973) 3-9.

My thanks go to the editors of these journals for kind permission to make use of these articles in the present book.

For Andrea and Stephanie

sirens of the North Fork

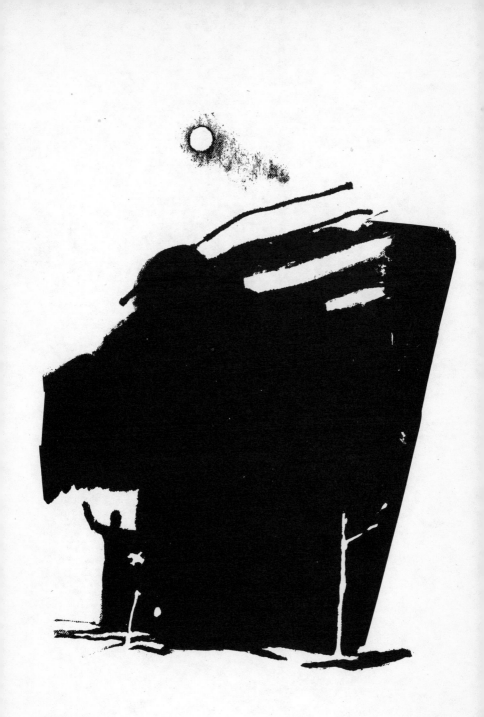

PART ONE

JESUS AS PRECURSOR

Jesus as Precursor

See For Yourself

Dusk was gathering rapidly, smells of the evening meal reached me from below, I dropped the paper in my lap and glanced out the window. An old friend, whom I recognized instantly by his characteristic gait and dress, was just turning the corner. I rushed down the stairs, rounded the corner blindly, nearly colliding with a policeman.

"I was hastening to catch a fellow — an old friend — who just passed this way," I said.

"No one has come this way," he replied: "See for yourself."

The street was empty. I looked bewildered at the blank faces of countless sleeping buildings. As I turned, the clock struck six. A milk truck rattled by. The first sun struck a roof in the distance. I could not identify the entrance to my apartment.

Jesus and Kafka

Jesus and Kafka

It may seem strange to augment the list of authorities on the parables of Jesus with the name of Franz Kafka. One is prompted to do so, initially, solely on account of Kafka's parable "On Parables," which stands appropriately first in the collection entitled, *Parables and Paradoxes.*

The first paragraph runs as follows:

> Many complain that the words of the wise are always merely parables and of no use in daily life, which is the only life we have. When the sage says: "Go over," he does not mean that we should cross to some actual place, which we could do anyhow if the labor were worth it; he means some fabulous yonder, something unknown to us, something too that he cannot designate more precisely, and therefore cannot help us here in the very least. And these parables really set out to say merely that the incomprehensible is incomprehensible, and we know that already. But the cares we have to struggle with every day: that is a different matter.

(11)

This paragraph delights those who agree that parables are

1

2   incomprehensible and useless. Others are puzzled and some angered because they think Kafka subverts the perfectly cogent and entirely lucid parable tradition they know. Still others — a few — are amused by the delight of the one group and the consternation of the other.

The second paragraph, to be considered momentarily, tends to sow confusion everywhere. But that is to anticipate.

"Many complain," we are told, "that the words of the wise are merely parables and of no use in daily life." The complaint itself represents a certain discernment. Those without complaint take the parables of the wise to have an ascertainable message translatable into non-parabolic language. The translation makes the parable applicable to everyday life. These are the swine before whom one should not cast pearls. The complainers, on the other hand, have some premonition that the parables have to do with the incomprehensible and so cannot be of any practical use.

Kafka obliges his readers to complain: he refuses any recognizable frame of reference for his work and thus compels his interpreters to speculate. The first hearers of Jesus apparently voiced a similar dissatisfaction, which is now "remembered" only obliquely in the tradition. Those habituated in the Christian tradition of interpretations take the parable to be a dispensable ornament for a prosaic point, long ago determined. That makes the tradition swinish. Kafka provides a gentle reminder that the parables of Jesus have been eclipsed by their interpretations: the maker of parables is known by the complaints he precipitates.

The initial complaint is linked to a second observation: when the sage says, "Go over," he does not refer to some actual place, but to a fabulous yonder. The prosaic mind is not interested in fabulous places unless they are real places, like Miami Beach or Disneyland. This fabulous place, moreover, is not here but "yonder," i.e. in some strange and perhaps exotic land, "away-from-here." And when the sage speaks of a fabulous yonder in parables, he apparently does so because he cannot designate it more precisely. In sum, the parable speaks of a *nowhere*, located *somewhere else*, in language intrinsically inexact.

It would be too much to suggest that the "kingdom of heaven" qualifies nicely under these rubrics.

The complaint of many is fully justified: parables are frustrating, if not maddening. The sage speaks of fabulous yonders of which he cannot be more precise. Why can he not be more precise? And why does he not address himself to common cares? When frustration borders on resignation, it is time to consider Kafka's second paragraph:

> Concerning this a man once said: Why such reluctance? If you
> only followed the parables you yourselves would become
> parables and with that rid of all your daily cares.
> Another said: I bet that is also a parable.
> The first said: You have won.
> The second said: But unfortunately only in parable.
> The first said: No, in reality; in parable you have lost.
>
> (11)

The first paragraph reflects a common frustration with parables where they have not been entirely domesticated. The second paragraph embodies this frustration. Students asked to write an interpretation of this paragraph often give up in utter perplexity; some drop the course in protest.

The second paragraph opens with an invitation, extended anonymously, to become a parable and with that be rid of daily cares. The response, also anonymous, is equivocal: rather than accepting or rejecting the invitation, this participant prefers to indulge in a game of definition. The invitation, he says, must itself be a parable!

This maneuver is designed to forestall the issue. It holds the question at arm's length while pretending to address it. The penultimate frustration of the rational mind is immanent: the definition or identification of the parable as parable is of no immediate or ultimate help; recognition is the homage the prosaic mind pays the sage from the safety of a habituated world. Even the slow learner will regularly come this far in the game: "I'll bet that is also a parable." It is crushing to discover that identification is a form of not-knowing, that recognition is the final refusal. The

4 parable must be seized as parable or not at all. The parable cannot
be reduced to other terms, not even when it is identified as parable.

The final frustration of rationality is to be wrong while being
right, to lose while winning. The second man has won his bet, but
unfortunately only in reality. And that is to suffer the loss of
parable, of that fabulous yonder, of the opportunity to divest
himself of daily cares.

The two final lines of dialogue make it clear that the parable, for
Kafka, does indeed have to do with a dispute over the "real," but a
dispute that transcends the literal. To have won in reality is to
remain bound to the everyday world, to daily cares, to be unable
to heed the invitation to "go over"; it also means to be imprisoned
in the literal. All of this is contrasted with the parable, with that
fabulous yonder, with the ability to cross over. Kafka does not
claim the word "reality" for the parable; he is content to issue an
invitation to vacate the real, i.e. the everyday, in favor of the
parabolic. To win in parable means to have shifted the locus of the
real.

Kafka sensed a steady and unblinking resistance to the parable,
to his work in general, which does not contain a literal word.
Although fascinated and even greatly amused by his stories,
friends and readers paused before whatever implications they felt
constrained to draw from them. This hesitation is expressed by the
opening sentence in paragraph two:

Concerning this a man once said: Why such reluctance? The
reluctance to "cross over" is given characteristic Kafkan voice in
the parable entitled "The Watchman":

> I ran past the first watchman. Then I was horrified, ran back
> again and said to the watchman: "I ran through here while you
> were looking the other way." The watchman gazed ahead of
> him and said nothing. "I suppose I really oughtn't to have done
> it," I said. The watchman still said nothing. "Does your silence
> indicate permission to pass?" . . .
>
> (*Parables and Paradoxes*: 81)

It is not enough that the way is open, that an invitation has been
issued, that the watchman is unseeing. The literal minds insists on

explicit permission to pass.

The reluctance to become parables is linked to the lack of explicitness, to the imprecision with which the sage speaks of that fabulous yonder. The parable has none of the allegorical transparency of *Pilgrim's Progress*; it is a poor road map for the traveler who has lost his way, particularly when the hour is late. To those who wish to place such demands on the parable, Kafka gives the recommendation to "Give It Up!" in this paragraph discovered among his papers upon his death:

> It was very early in the morning, the streets clean and deserted, I was on my way to the railroad station. As I compared the tower clock with my watch I realized it was already much later than I had thought, I had to hurry, the shock of this discovery made me feel uncertain of the way, I was not very well acquainted with the town as yet, fortunately there was a policeman nearby, I ran to him and breathlessly asked him the way. He smiled and said: "From me you want to learn the way?" "Yes," I said, "since I cannot find it myself." "Give it up, give it up," said he, and turned away with a great sweep, like someone who wants to be alone with his laughter.
>
> (Politzer: 1)

There is a great humor in the refusal to give directions — a humor that goes with the riddle of the way already set before the traveler. In this riddle, the destination is clearly indicated, but maps, guides, advance reservations are useless; the journey is too immense.

> I gave orders for my horse to be brought round from the stable. The servant did not understand me. I myself went to the stable, saddled my horse and mounted. In the distance I heard a bugle call, I asked him what this meant. He knew nothing and had heard nothing. At the gate he stopped me, asking: "Where are you riding to, master?" "I don't know," I said, "only away from here, away from here. Always away from here, only by doing so can I reach my destination." "And so you know your destination?" he asked. "Yes," I answered, "didn't I say so? Away-From-Here, that is my destination." "You have no provisions with you," he said. "I need none," I said, "the journey is so long that I must die of hunger if I don't get

6   anything on the way. No provisions can save me. For it is,
fortunately, a truly immense journey."

(*Parables and Paradoxes*: 189)

That fabulous yonder is away-from-here; those who would reach
it must set out from where they are — without provisions, and
without directions.

This talk about immense journeys, giving it up, unseeing and
unhearing watchmen — if we may pause for a backward
glance — undoubtedly appears unrelated to and remote from the
parables of Jesus. One might ask, in fact, whether Kafka has
anything at all to say about Jesus. The answer to that question can
only be, certainly not. To which I hasten to add: that is the best
reason for invoking Kafka in contemplating Jesus.

Although Kafka has nothing to say about Jesus, the two men
are nevertheless related. The curious will be struck by four
remarkable affinities: both men were displaced Jews; both wrote
or spoke in an alien tongue (if Jesus did not speak Greek, we must
give the name Jesus to the composer of the parables and
aphorisms in the gospel tradition); both anticipated a holocaust;
both were makers of parables. Brothers often have less to bind
them together. However, I remark these affinities only in passing.

To return to the previous point: perhaps the only sound reason
for considering Kafka in connection with Jesus is to divert
attention from the clamor of traditional voices that drowns out
the voice of Jesus. Jesus is relieved of the burden of his
interpreters, so to speak, for the brief time he sojourns in the
shadow of Kafka. This might transpire, for example, during a
course of lectures ostensibly treating both men but in fact making
reference only to the one. The anticipation that the other man will
be spoken of is constantly frustrated; this has an emptying effect,
if persisted in, like the practice of zazen.

It may be argued that, for this purpose, any interesting writer
will do. Unfortunately, that is not the case. For the one author to
be effectively distractive with respect to the other, the one must be
proximally distractive. That is, the one must skirt, penetrate, or
traverse the territory essentially occupied by the other.

Distraction occasioned by the new or novel merely shifts attention and will not produce catharsis; proximal distraction, by contrast, is redemptive of what is eclipsed.

The question of Kafka and Jesus should therefore be put differently: is Jesus in any fundamental sense a *precursor* of Kafka?

The Argentine writer, Jorge Luis Borges, has declared, in an essay on Kafka, "the fact is that each writer *creates* his own precursors" (*Other Inquisitions*: 108). Borges was at first inclined to the view that Kafka was as singular as the Phoenix; then he came to see that Kafka had many precursors. Kafka's precursors have little in common among themselves; it is only in Kafka that they are brought together, only in him that their affinities come to light. This is because Kafka modifies the way we read his precursors; had Kafka not taught us to read them, we would not know the real tradition to which they belong.

Borges does not include Jesus among the precursors of Kafka. Among others, he identifies Zeno, Han Yu, Kierkegaard, Robert Browning, but not the Nazarene. The omission is curious, especially when one notices that Jesus, Kafka and Borges are among the few great tellers of parables in the West. It is just possible that the omission is deliberate.

I make this suggestion at the prompting of Borges himself. In his short story entitled, "The Garden of Forking Paths," two men are discussing a novel called "The Garden of Forking Paths." One is a descendant of the famous Chinese general who had written the novel, the other a renowned Sinologist. It is known that the general, a philosopher and mystic, was preoccupied all his life with the problem of time. Yet his novel, which contains much abstruse metaphysical speculation and on which he labored for thirteen years, never refers to the problem of time. Indeed, time is never mentioned. The two discussants are pondering this strange fact. The Sinologist asks the other:

> "In a riddle whose answer is chess, what is the only prohibited word?"
> I thought a moment and replied, "The word *chess*."

"Precisely," said Albert. "The Garden of Forking Paths" is an enormous riddle, whose theme is time; this hidden reason prohibits its mention."

(Labyrinths: 27, modified)

For this reason, it is possible that Borges was also interested in Jesus as a precursor of Kafka, but felt that direct reference to Jesus would thwart not only his interest in Jesus but his concern to locate Kafka also.

This may also be the reason Kafka has nothing to say about Jesus, and the reason Jesus does not refer to Moses in *his* parables.

It is of course absurd to claim that books written about certain subjects are in fact books about other subjects, although that is sometimes the case. Owen Barfield reports the story of a perplexed author who lacked a title for his book. A friend asked him, "Do you make any reference to angels? Any reference to trumpets?" "No?" "Then, why not call it, 'No Angels, No Trumpets'?" But we are speaking here of parables and makers of parables. In a parable whose answer is "the Kingdom of God," that is the forbidden subject matter. In a parable whose answer is "the parables of Jesus," *that* is the forbidden topic.

We are left, consequently, with the question whether Kafka is proximally distractive with reference to Jesus. That question can only be answered concretely: does Kafka modify the way we read Jesus? Is Jesus a bona fide precursor of Kafka? Conversely, is Kafka one of the authentic successors to whom Jesus gives rise? If the answer is "yes," the discussion of the parables of Kafka with which this essay began is entirely appropriate, and Kafka's parables are materially related to the parables of Jesus. In that case, nothing further need be said. If Kafka does not "create" Jesus as a precursor, the discussion has been futile.

A Pair of Trees:
Jesus and Beckett

The Willow Tree is for Hanging
The Looking-Glass Tree is for the Birds
In Place of Questions

The Willow Tree is for Hanging
Samuel Beckett: Waiting for Godot

When Samuel Beckett's *Waiting for Godot* was first performed in Paris, January, 1953, a fist fight broke out in the lobby during intermission. The altercation was prophetic: one may fight with Beckett, or one may embrace him, but it is hard simply to wait, motionless, inert, indifferent. Perhaps that is because in his work modern man recognizes himself, either as that self he blindly and violently resists, or as that self he knows he must accredit to remain sane. In either case Becket speaks profoundly to the present age. His work, *Godot* in particular, provides a remarkably illuminating index to the contemporary world: its empty language, its vain hope, its absurdity.

I

The two principals of the play, Estragon, whose stage name is Gogo, and Vladimir, whose stage name is Didi, confess, repeatedly, to be waiting for Godot. The predominant activity in which they are engaged for more than an hour, in fact, is waiting.

12   Time flows through and around them without biting into their being: at the end of Act I they are just where they began, and Act II is a repetition of Act I. Had Beckett written a third act, it would have recapitulated the first two and the audience would have run out screaming. The wait of Gogo and Didi is thus cyclical, marked only by the alternation of day and night. This vicious circularity is also thematic with Eugene Ionesco, whose plays, *The Bald Soprano* and *The Lesson*, begin all over again before the final curtain.

The boredom of idle conversation is relieved to a certain extent by the appearance of a second pair, Pozzo and Lucky. But this hapless master and his slave are no better off than Gogo and Didi. They have come from nowhere and are going nowhere. The repetitiousness of the action — or lack of it — is symbolized by Lucky's hilarious business with his baggage. Each time he is given an order by Pozzo, he must put down his load, one piece at a time — whip, folding stool, picnic basket, overcoat, and suitcase filled with sand — execute the order, and then laboriously retrieve his gear, again one object at a time.

Gogo and Didi are waiting, as remarked, for Godot. Godot, of course, does not appear, but at the end of each act a messenger, a boy, arrives to tell the pair that Godot will not come today but surely tomorrow. The boy — who appears to be the same boy on these two and other occasions, but who claims he is not — does not seem to recognize Gogo and Didi from one time to the next. He is a goatherd in the service of Godot; he has a brother who is a shepherd and who apparently is either not in favor with Godot — Godot beats him — or is sick. The message, however, whether delivered by the same or different boys, is perpetually the same: not today, but most certainly tomorrow.

The stage is simply set: a country road, a single, barren tree of sorts, nothing else. It is evening.

II

The monotone and monochrome impression produced by the play is very skillfully wrought. The audience does not know whether to laugh or be horrified by the tedium laden with suspense. And suspense-laden it is. The monotony is pervaded by a vague hope, by an evanescent anticipation, that persists through and beyond the play. Those who leave at the end of the First Act, leave not because they are bored, but because they are incensed. The rest remain and debate whether Godot will ever come.

The persistence of hope — or habit — is typified by the sequence at the end of each Act, a sequence that is repeated, in other forms, numerous times during the course of the play. Didi and Gogo agree once again, at the close of Act II, to leave.

> Vladimir: Well? Shall we go?
> Estragon: Yes, let's go.
> Stage direction: *They do not move.*   (60)

The tedium is relieved, or penetrated, by other, relatively minor and obscure events, which indicate a certain marginal temporal passage within the two days encompassed by the play. These events, or developments, easily escape the eye.

Gogo's boots, for example, mysteriously fit him in Act II, whereas they were the source of much discomfort in Act I. In Act II Pozzo goes blind, and Lucky, who danced and recited in the First Act, has become dumb. However, another very modest mark of temporal progression invites attention, since it is to this mark that the hope of Didi and Gogo appears to be especially related. Yet it is an ambiguous sign. One might even say: it is at once the very slender basis of hope and the symbol of futility, of absurdity, perhaps even of ultimate disillusionment.

Early in the first act, Estragon announces that he wants to go. Vladimir replies that they can't. And why? asks Estragon.

> Vladimir: We're waiting for Godot.
> Estragon: (*despairingly*). Ah! (*Pause*) You're sure it was here?

14

Vladimir:	What?
Estragon:	That we were to wait.
Vladimir:	He said by the tree. (*They look at the tree.*) Do you see any others? (10)

The tree, then, is the locus of their waiting. Momentarily their attention is drawn to the tree and the dialogue continues:

Estragon:	What is it?
Vladimir:	I don't know. A willow.
Estragon:	Where are the leaves?
Vladimir:	It must be dead.
Estragon:	No more weeping.
Vladimir:	Or perhaps it's not the season.
Estragon:	Looks to me more like a bush.
Vladimir:	A shrub.
Estragon:	A bush.
Vladimir:	A — . What are you insinuating? That we've come to the wrong place?
Estragon:	He should be here.
Vladimir:	He didn't say for sure he'd come.
Estragon:	And if he doesn't come?
Vladimir:	We'll come back to-morrow.
Estragon:	And then the day after to-morrow.
Vladimir:	Possibly.
Estragon:	And so on. (10)

This exchange is very suggestive. Gogo and Didi are not able to identify the tree with certainty, but Didi thinks it may be a willow. In any case, the tree is barren. This may mean that the willow weeps no more, or that it may not be the season for leaves. The latter recalls the cursing of the fig tree in the Gospels; there the fig tree had leaves but no fruit, as it was not the season (Mk 11:12-14, 20-25; Mt 21:18-19, 20-22).

Gogo and Didi apparently agree that it may not qualify as a tree at all, but dispute whether it is a bush or a shrub. This dispute may be an allusion to the parable of the mustard seed (Mk 4:30-32; Mt 13:31-32; Lk 13:18-19), which, as reported in the Gospels, contains an interesting discrepancy: the Evangelists disagree as to whether the mustard is a tree or a shrub.

That Beckett was acutely aware of discrepancies in the Gospels

is evidenced by Vladimir's musings on the two thieves crucified
with Jesus. One of the Evangelists says that one thief was saved;
another says that both abused Jesus; two do not mention the
thieves at all. Why believe one Evangelist rather than the other?
asks Didi (8f.).

Beckett's conflation of motifs from the cursing of the fig tree
and the parable of the mustard seed is paralleled by a curious link
in the Gospels themselves: the saying about faith so as to move
mountains, linked in the Gospels to the cursing of the fig tree (Mk
11:23; Mt 21:21), is reported elsewhere by Matthew as the saying
about having faith as *a grain of mustard seed* so as to move
mountains (Mt 17:20), a saying which is given a third form in
Luke: "If you had faith as a grain of mustard seed, you could say
to this sycamine tree, 'Be rooted up, and be planted in the sea,' and
it would obey you" (Lk 17:6). The motifs of the barren tree, the
mustard seed, and faith to move mountains or trees, so oddly
interlocked in the Gospels, seems to have caught the imagination
of Beckett.

In the parable, the kingdom of God is likened to a mustard
plant. It is a strange metaphor. Is it possible that the tree, or shrub,
or bush, in *Godot*, as the locus of waiting and thus of hope, also
symbolizes redemption? Is that miserable dead tree the tree of life,
the cross, stationed at the navel of the earth?

Meanwhile, Gogo and Didi have a tiff over a dream and a story,
fall out, and then are reconciled. Didi asks, "What do we do now?"
Gogo responds, "Wait." "Yes, but while waiting?" "What about
hanging ourselves?" suggests Gogo. This practical proposal can
scarcely be implemented without the complicity of the tree, so the
two consider whether the bough of the tree will bear their weight.
Unable to decide which is the heavier — to determine who would
go first — they resume waiting.

> Vladimir: Let's wait and see what he says.
> Estragon: Who?
> Vladimir: Godot.
> Estragon: Good idea. (12)

Near the end of Act I their interest in hanging themselves from

16 the tree is briefly revived. But they haven't the necessary bit of rope.

Estragon: Remind me to bring a bit of rope tomorrow.
Vladimir: Yes. Come on. (35)

III

In the stage directions for Act II, the author orders the tree to sprout four or five leaves. Gogo does not notice the difference. In fact, he does not even remember the tree. "That's the way I am," he says. "Either I forget immediately or I never forget" (39). A little later he proclaims, "I'm not a historian" (42). Didi, however, remarks the change and endeavors to call Gogo's attention to it. Gogo insists that Didi must have dreamt the tree (39, 42).

Vladimir: Do you not remember?
Estragon: I'm tired.
Vladimir: Look at it.
They look at the tree.
Estragon: I see nothing.
Vladimir: But yesterday evening it was all black and bare. And now it's covered with leaves.
Estragon: Leaves?
Vladimir: In a single night.
Estragon: It must be Spring.
Vladimir: But in a single night!
Estragon: I tell you we weren't here yesterday. Another of your nightmares. (42)

As in Act I, so again at the close of Act II, after the sun has set and the moon risen, Didi and Gogo note that Godot has not come. Gogo inquires: "And if we dropped him?"

Vladimir: He'd punish us. (*Silence. He looks at the tree.*) Everything's dead but the tree.
Estragon: (*looking at the tree*) What is it?
Vladimir: It's the tree.
Estragon: Yes, but what kind?
Vladimir: I don't know. A willow.
Estragon draws Vladimir towards the tree. They stand motionless before it. Silence.

    Estragon: Why don't we hang ourselves?
    Vladimir: With what?
    Estragon: You haven't got a bit of rope?
    Vladimir: No.
    Estragon: Then we can't.
      Silence.

At this point Gogo remembers his belt. He withdraws it, his pants fall to the ground, and the pair test the frayed cord to see whether it will hold them. It breaks.

    Estragon: You say we have to come back to-morrow?
    Vladimir: Yes.
    Estragon: Then we can bring a good bit of rope.
    Vladimir: Yes.
      Silence.

* * *

    Vladimir: We'll hang ourselves to-morrow. (Pause.) Unless
             Godot comes.
    Estragon: And if he comes?
    Vladimir: We'll be saved.   (59f.)

IV

Gogo, as we have noticed, accuses Vladimir of dreaming things — things Gogo cannot remember. Vladimir, on the other hand, is deathly afraid of dreams — and stories. So afraid that he won't let Gogo recite his stories or confide his dreams.

Gogo has fallen asleep on the mound. Didi calls him: "Gogo! . . . Gogo! . . . GOGO!"

    Estragon: I was asleep! (*Despairingly.*) Why will you never let
             me sleep?
    Vladimir: I felt lonely.
    Estragon: I had a dream.
    Vladimir: Don't tell me!
    Estragon: I dreamt that —
    Vladimir: DON'T TELL ME!
    Estragon: (*gesture toward the universe.*) This one is enough
             for you?   (11)

The Looking-Glass Tree is for the Birds
Jesus: The Parable of the Mustard Seed

I

The mighty cedars of Lebanon crown a magnificent spine of mountains strung casually along the shores of the eastern Mediterranean. The snowclad peaks fall away proudly and precipitously into the azure waters of the sea on the one side, and into the flat, burning mirror of the desert on the other. Riding this haughty crest, sandwiched between water and waste, the muscle-bound trunk of the cedar silently announces its stately grandeur. The cedar does not want for nourishment or for admiration, nor does it want for those who, like Solomon, covet its splendid timber.

Few Israelites could fail to be impressed by the towering height and bulk of the Lebanese cedar. Ezekiel was no exception. So impressive did he find it that it inspired one of his rich metaphors (Ezek 17:22-24).

From the lofty top of the cedar — so Ezekiel's vision runs — Yahweh will take a tender twig, which he will plant on a high and lofty mountain, on the mountain height of Israel. Under the surveillance of the Lord God, the young cedar will wax and

20 mature, will put forth boughs and bear fruit. It will furnish a haven for beasts of every kind, and the birds of the heaven will make their nests in the shade of its branches.

The noble cedar, seemingly immovable, from a human perspective apparently eternal, symbolizes the secular powers of the earth. From among the tender shoots of its majestic imperturbability, Yahweh will take the tenderest and from it produce a new cedar to be the glory of Israel. The cedar of Israel, which will form the locus of eschatological rest for all the peoples of the earth, will stem from the lineage of the secular powers: Yahweh will create his cedar out of the stock of the secular cedar, but will make it serve his own redemptive purposes.

Since the cedar of Israel will exceed the secular cedars in nobility and grandeur, in strength and longevity, all the trees of the field shall know that Yahweh brings the high tree low and exalts the low tree, that he dries up the green tree and causes the withered tree to flourish. The lone cedar of Israel will displace the secular cedars, which will pale, by comparison, into insignificance.

Thus the word of the Lord God in the mouth of Ezekiel: the Lord has spoken, and he will do it.

II

The parable of the mustard seed (Mk 4:30-32) is undoubtedly to be read against the background of the history of the symbol of the mighty cedar, a symbol utilized not only by Ezekiel, but found also in Daniel 4 and elsewhere in the Old Testament. The interplay of Jesus' parable and the tradition has to be considered initially, however, in connection with the history of recent interpretation. Only in this way can the full range of metaphorical overtones be discerned by ears atuned to prespecified wave lengths.

The emphasis on the smallness of the seed — "the smallest seed in the world" — found in parentheses in Mark (4:31b) and echoed by Matthew (13:32) and the Gospel of Thomas (20), is taken by C. H. Dodd to be a secondary expansion of the parable. Luke's version, which omits this emphasis and is assumed to derive from Q, is held to be original. The parable has nothing to do with the contrast between insignificant beginnings and great issue, according to Dodd, but with the capacity of the shrub to afford shelter to the birds of the heavens. The parable therefore announces that the time has come when the multitudes of Israel, perhaps even of the Gentiles, will flock to the kingdom as birds flock to the shelter of the tree (Dodd: 191).

It is quite possible that Mark's parenthesis, and thus the emphasis on the minute size of the seed, is secondary, as Dodd thinks. However, Dodd fails to notice that the seed in question is the mustard seed in every form of the tradition, and the microscopic size of this seed, with or without emphasis, was already proverbial.

The oversight of Dodd coincides with an aberration of the original parable to be found already in the New Testament itself: in Mark (4:32) the seed grows into the greatest of all *shrubs*, but in Matthew (13:32) and Luke (13:19) it becomes a *tree*. It is hardly speculation to say that the eschatological tree of Ezekiel and Daniel has influenced the transmission of the parable in the New Testament period, and that it has also shaped Dodd's perspective.

The theological interest in making the parable conform to the prophetic and apocalyptic tradition has thus been at work on the one side, in the tendency to play down the smallness of the seed and play up the size of the mature plant.

Modern botanical interests have joined the game, on the other side, in an attempt to salvage the "realism" of the parable. Rather than have the birds come and *make their nests* in the branches of a shrub, the botanizers want the birds to "light upon" or "roost" in its branches. It is of course the case that only Matthew and Luke speak of birds dwelling in the *branches*; in Mark's version the birds are able to make their nests in the shade of the shrub, while Thomas has it that a large branch becomes a shelter for birds. The botanists know that mustard does not grow to tree size, although it may reach a height of 8 or 10 feet. It is an annual plant, moreover, which, although fast growing, and consequently

22   mostly hollow, would hardly provide nesting places for birds in
the early spring. It seems more reasonable, then, from a botanical
point of view, to say that birds come and "roost" in the mustard
plant during summer, attracted seasonally, as they are, to its shade
and to its seed.

The text, however, is everywhere clear: birds come and *dwell* in
or under the shrub. Whether preferred or not, the parable indulges
in a bit of exaggeration, hyperbole, if you will, which every
common hearer, who might have been expected to know
something of the mustard plant first hand, would scarcely have
missed: foolish birds to take up their abode in the short-lived
mustard!

The difficulties inherent in the parable merely illustrate how
poorly suited the figure is to the old cedar imagery on the one
hand, and to modern botanical exactness on the other. The
botanists are interested, of course, in saving the everyday
literalness of the parable. Modern theological interpreters, under
the spell of Daniel 4, Ezekiel 17 and 31, are interested in asserting
the literal figurativeness of the parable. The interpretation of
Joachim Jeremias illustrates the second position well, when he
writes of the parables of the Mustard Seed and Leaven as parables
of contrast:

> Their meaning is that out of the most insignificant
> beginnings, invisible to the human eye, God creates his mighty
> Kingdom, which embraces all the people of the earth.
>
> (149; cf. Dodd: 190)

The mighty kingdom is symbolized by the "mighty" mustard
plant, which provides a haven for birds from the four corners of
the heavens! Jeremias has recapitulated Ezekiel's allegory of the
cedar of Israel, with hardly a glance in the direction of the parable
of the mustard seed.

III

Dodd sees the parable as depicting the growth of the tree up to
the point where it can shelter birds (190). It is therefore an
announcement that the period of obscurity for Jesus is at an end.

Jeremias thinks that the parable sets out the fundamental contrast between the beginning and end of a process, which, he claims, is the oriental way of viewing a story. He therefore takes the parable to affirm the miraculous power of God in the face of doubts that the kingdom could issue from the mission of Jesus and his disreputable band.

Of the two, Jeremias more nearly seizes the parable as a whole, but he, too, finally comes to rest in the shade of the noble cedar.

The metaphorical meanings assigned by Dodd and Jeremias to the parable represent what might be called first octave metaphorical overtones. It is not so much that these overtones are false notes in themselves, as that they are not being heard in concert with second and third octave metaphorical overtones, which is to say that the parable is not being heard as a whole in relation to the history of the imagery.

When the parable of Jesus is set alongside the vision of Ezekiel (17:22-24), the first impression one gains by the juxtaposition is that Jesus has created a light-hearted burlesque of Ezekiel's figure: the noble cedar, which provides a haven for the beasts and birds of the earth, is caricatured as a lowly mustard plant! And the first impression is not entirely wide of the mark. At second glance, however, the parable takes on the character of serious satire. Jesus appears to have grasped the final injunction of Ezekiel's oracle radically, "The Lord will bring the high tree low and make the low tree high"! The noble cedar of Israel, as the hope of Israel, will be quite comparable, on Ezekiel's view, to the secular cedars of the world. But when Jesus takes up the figure, it is to conform Ezekiel's new cedar — precisely Israel's future — to Yahweh's final dictum. That is only to say that all cedars, including Israel's proud hope, will be brought low, and the insignificant tree, indeed the ephemeral mustard plant, will be made to bear Israel's true destiny.

The kingdom as Jesus sees it breaking in will arrive in disenchanting and disarming form: not as a mighty cedar astride the lofty mountain height but as a lowly garden herb. The kingdom is asserted with comic relief: what it is and what it will

24   do, it will be and do, appearances to the contrary notwithstanding. It will erupt out of the power of weakness and refuse to perpetuate itself by the weakness of power.

The mustard plant does offer a refuge to the birds of heaven, but what a modest refuge it is — in the eyes of the world! The contrast between insignificant beginning and glorious end is a pittance paid to the grandiose pretensions of human hope. Man asks for a continent as the paradisiacal sanctuary of his final rest and is given a clump of earth. The birds, too, have their metaphorical wings clipped: what odd birds they are to flock — in modest numbers — to the shade of a seasonal plant, thinking it to be their eternal home.

If the kingdom is extended in the parable with comic relief, it is in order to offer the kingdom only for what it is. It is not a towering empire, but an unpretentious venture of faith. As a venture of faith, however, it is of course potentially world-transforming: "If you have faith as a grain of mustard seed, you will say to the mountain, 'Move hence to yonder place,' and it will move" (Mt 17:20). It is faith which, in its unostentatious way, reorders the face of the world.

The parable relocates the power of the kingdom where the world cannot have access to it apart from faith. The parable is full of promise and assurance, but these become available only in the context of what the kingdom really is, viz: the faith to dwell in the kingdom.

IV

The parable of the mustard seed intends nothing less than to transform the face of Israel's hope. The transformation of a tradition is much like moving mountains by word of command: both are equally difficult to effect because both are dependent upon the power of words. Hope and mountains belong to the map of reality which man takes to be fixed and unalterable. Because of his god-like tenacity in clinging to what presents itself as stubborn reality, man finds world-transforming faith difficult to negotiate:

he prefers a literal world, the order of which is immutable, to a
world subject to the linguistic whims of the poet and prophet, and
thus open to the future.

Among those to whom the parable of the mustard seed was
addressed were those who reckoned their chances of participating
in Israel's hope, as traditionally understood, to be good. It was too
much to expect them to abandon a reasonably certain future for
themselves, even if they had to purchase that future at the expense
of most other men. The risk was too great for them to be lured
away by the ludicrous vision of an idle blasphemer. Those who
had no future and no prospect of one, on the other hand, were no
doubt favorably disposed to a fresh pack of cards and a new deal,
if not a new frontier. Any prospect at all was better than none. Yet
they, too, found it difficult to risk the future, such as it was, on
such a hazardous gamble. It must have been like inviting them to
flee the debtor's prison and gallows by taking a leaky, short-
masted, poorly provisioned frigate for the new world, on the
condition that they would welcome aboard all and sundry who
wanted to go, and face the prospect of an endless voyage at sea.
There were few, even among the destitute, who were desperate
enough to set out. Such is the power of the old hope that besets the
human breast, even when that hope is certainly beyond reach.

The church, like Israel, is wont to stumble over its hope. It
seizes, solidifies, and then takes possession of its hope in the name
of divinely certified reality. In so doing, it merely converts the
mustard plant back into a towering cedar. As regards that hope
and its encapsulation in the tradition, the parable suggests the
following items for reflection:

1. Whatever the Christian hope is, the form of its realization
will come as a surprise to all who think they know what it ought to
be.

2. The coming of the kingdom will disappoint the righteous,
but be a source of joy to the religiously disinherited.

3. The certainty of hope is inversely proportionate to the
certainty with which the resurrection of Jesus is held to be
paradigmatic of the future.

4. The promise of the future is directly proportionate to the degree that one makes no claim upon the future at all.

5. The gift of the future is the gift of language: the mystery of the divine promise is tendered in and through language, and it is seized and lived into as the salvific word occurring between and among men.

Jesus advances the parable as an invitation to pass through the looking-glass: on the other side the mighty cedar is brought low and the humble herb exalted. On the other side: that is to say, in the world mirrored in the looking-glass of the parable.

The Willow Tree Is for Hanging/
The Looking-Glass Tree is for the Birds

In Place of Questions

1.1   In an absurd world the question of meaning is irrelevant.

1.2   In a parabolic world the question of meaning is pre-empted.

1.3   In a mundane world the question of meaning is reduced to the question of words.

2.1   In the modern mundane world language has died a torturous death: it has been stretched on the rack of propaganda and starved in the dungeon of gossip.

2.2   In the world of absurd theatre language is a millstone about the neck: it deadens the optic nerves.

2.3   In the parables of Jesus language opens onto a greater reality.

3.1   With Jesus language happens: to him, to his hearers, to the world.

3.2   With Mr. Everyman language is a vicious circle.

3.3   With Absurd Man language deadens and ossifies: it does not happen, it persists.

28 4.1   In the absurd world, order is vanquished by chaos.

4.2   In the parabolic world, the mundane order is inverted.

4.3   In the mundane world, order is a mind-set gone to seed.

5.1   In the everyday world, comedy is blasphemous.

5.2   In the parabolic world, comedy is redeeming.

5.3   In the absurd world, comedy is tragic.

6.1   In the world of absurdities, resurrection, were it contemplated at all, would be tragic, that is, hell.

6.2   In the world of everydayness, resurrection is deemed the perpetuation of the *status quo* for those with status; for those without status, it is the reversal of rank.

6.3   In the world of the parable, resurrection is not anticipated, except as a farce: a fate commensurate with the pretentions that underlie the aspiration.

7.0   The mundane mind trivializes parables by moralizing them, but in an absurd world parables have died because imagination, meaning and metaphor have atrophied. Beckett weeps at the open grave; the congregation sings, "Christ the Lord is risen today!"

Away-From-Here as the Destination:

Jesus and: Henry Miller Carlos Castaneda

From Priest to Artist: Away-From-Here as the
Destination
The Parable of the Leaven: Away-From-Here as
the Destination

Away-From-Here as the Destination

My Destination

I gave order for my horse to be brought round from the stable. The servant did not understand me. I myself went to the stable, saddled my horse and mounted. In the distance I heard a bugle call, I asked him what this meant. He knew nothing and had heard nothing. At the gate he stopped me, asking: "Where are you riding to, master?" "I don't know," I said, "only away from here, away from here. Always away from here, only by doing so can I reach my destination." "And so you know your destination?" he asked. "Yes," I answered, "didn't I say so? Away-From-Here, that is my destination." "You have no provisions with you," he said. "I need none," I said, "the journey is so long that I must die of hunger if I don't get anything on the way. No provisions can save me. For it is, fortunately, a truly immense journey."

Parables and Paradoxes: 189

From Priest to Artist:
Away-From-Here as the Destination

The foundations of the counter culture have been laid by an invasion of centaurs, according to Theodore Roszak (42f.). What are the "foundations"? The foundations are the non-intellective powers that call into question all that our culture values as "reason" and "reality" (54f.). In other terms, the foundations consist of a new vision of the real that is pre-intellective (but not non-intellective): a vision that contests the validity of what is taken, by the reigning mentality, to be the real and reasonable. Who, then, are the centaurs? The centaurs are the intruders — half man, half beast — who challenge the proprieties of civilization. And, of course, it is Apollo, the god of reason and culture, who opposes the centaurs.

John Updike named one of his novels *The Centaur*. In it he traces the "degeneration" of the Caldwell family. The end term of that degeneration is the artist. The link Updike posits between the artistic imagination and the invasion of centaurs is suggestive. It is worth exploring through the eyes of a writer who aspired to be an artist — and a centaur — more than four decades ago.

34

I

"Priest, teacher, artist — the classic degeneration" wrote John Updike in his novel, *The Centaur*, with reference to the three generations of the family he depicts there. The declension is suitable to more than the Caldwell family: it characterizes an age. The desertion of the priesthood has already passed into the common consciousness; the evidence suggests that even now we are in the transition from teacher to artist.

What does this degeneration signal? In a general way and with a certain deliberate imprecision it may be said that it signals a historical breach of immense proportions. Not a breach, to be sure, as clearly marked as the invention of the wheel, the victory of the Greeks at Thermopylae, the fall of Rome, or the splitting of the atom. Rather, it is a breach that remains largely hidden, that is discernible only indirectly in the consequent disruption it produces. It is a breach that is on its way, so to speak, and which, even in retrospect, will probably never be localized to the degree that we now presume to locate the turn of the ages in Jesus of Nazareth. Yet there are certain parallels, such as initial anonymity and obscurity, that are suggestive.

This breach Nietzsche names the "death of God." He of course had the previous two thousand years of Western history in view when he chose the rubric. As significant as its Nietzschean name may be, it is more to the point to notice how he depicts its *kairos*:

> At last he [the madman] threw his lantern on the ground, and it broke and went out. "I come too early," he said then; "my time has not come yet. This tremendous event is still on its way, still wandering — it has not yet reached the ears of man. Lightning and thunder require time, the light of the stars requires time, deeds require time even after they are done, before they can be seen and heard. This deed is still more distant from them than the most distant stars — *and yet they have done it themselves*."
>
> (96)

Nietzsche died in 1900: the event was still on its way, even then no nearer than the stars, *yet it had already occurred.*

Franz Kafka died in 1924: in his parable, *The Imperial Message*, the message had already been dispatched by the dying emperor, the messenger had begun to wend his way out of the castle, yet the innumerable multitudes, the endless chambers, corridors, stairs, court yards, gates make it impossible that he will be able to deliver it to you, even after a thousand years. In the meantime the emperor has died. As certain as you are that the messenger is on his way, you have no choice but sit at the window at evening and dream its contents to yourself (*Parables and Paradoxes*: 13ff.).

Nietzsche's madman arrived ahead of his time, as prophets often do. He threw his lantern to the ground and its light went out. The disjunction between the time of his time and his time was too great for rational thought to bear. Kafka is no longer perplexed by the disjunction; he merely takes it for granted and contemplates it without so much as a literal word, without so much as a prediction or protest, with only the serene assurance that it has arrived unheralded.

The time of the time is foreshadowed in Nietzsche. In Kafka it is incarnate. In the idol of the post World War II world, Albert Camus, the time for prophecy has come and gone, the time for embodiment is already past. It is time to reckon with the time of the time. He writes in the *Myth of Sisyphus*, "There is no fate that cannot be surmounted by scorn" (121). And scorn is sufficient to surmount a world shorn of its ancient rationale. Even to Sisyphus, condemned to perpetual fruitless labor, "This Universe henceforth without a master seems . . . neither sterile nor futile" (123).

In Nietzsche, Kafka, Camus, a period is being set to the end of an era and another epoch opened. They represent Updike's classic degeneration as premature manifestations of its end term. They state the basis of the degeneration. They discerned, however dimly, the time of the time. They caught sight of the gross hiatus opening between them and the "world," the tradition, they had inherited. The historical breach of immense proportions yawned

36 before them. If what to them seemed so self-evident, so irrefragable, so inevitable, has not yet passed into the common consciousness, no matter. The momentous event arrived silently, unannounced. On the other hand, neither they nor the event has failed to leave its mark here and there, perhaps especially where it is least expected.

II

It will be illuminating to consider what the term artist in Updike's triad denotes. Illuminating because it will suggest why the degeneration has taken the direction it has. Who and what the artist is will also indicate the character of the historical disjunction that constitutes the time of the time.

For the artist emerging between the two great wars Henry Miller may serve as the paradigm. He will serve not only because he is an index to the genus, but also because he explicitly identifies himself in both the *Tropic of Cancer* and the *Tropic of Capricorn*, thus sparing the pain and the risk of conclusion by analysis.

The declension, priest-teacher-artist, is a trajectory that signals the pursuit of the "real." The "real" is the "really real," as opposed to the allegedly real. The pursuit of the "real" is prompted by the conviction that what is real is not what is commonly taken to be real. The quest of the real is thus grounded in the circumspection that the "world" of Mr. Everyman is phony, a cardboard stage on which he acts out his role in the common comedy, the script for which the received tradition has already fixed. The center of gravity in the literature and art of our time is that the received "world" is a grand farce, a make-believe construction saturated with illusion from top to bottom. To this conviction Henry Miller gives poignant expression:

> The whole [American] continent is sound asleep and in that
> sleep a grand nightmare is taking place.
>
> (*Tropic of Capricorn*: 42)

Sleep is an even greater danger than that insomnia called "living,"
according to Miller. In order to avoid both sleep and insomnia,
there are those masquerading as artists who string words endlessly
together for the purpose of staying awake. But Miller aspires to
wakefulness without props; he yearns to be in touch with "the
degenerate remnants of earlier races of man who . . . must have
had a greater hold on reality" (323).

Like so many novelists and poets of this century, Miller regards
himself as entirely alienated from the received world:

> To the life about me, to the people who made up the world I
> knew, I could not attach my signature, I was as definitely
> outside their world as a cannibal is outside the bounds of
> civilized society.
>
> (54)

Miller's alienation is acute because the world he once knew is dead
(225), and the new reality to which he must attempt to give himself
does not yet exist, it is still far, far away (225f.). Yet he is certain
that it is there: "I may walk from now till doomsday with head
down and never find it. But it is there, I am sure of it" (226).

Any move toward the new reality entails a radical and absolute
rejection of the old world:

> Even if I must become a wild and natural park inhabited only
> by idle dreamers I must not stop to rest here in the ordered
> fatuity of responsible, adult life. I must do this . . . in
> remembrance of the life of a child who was strangled and stifled
> by the mutual consent of those who had surrendered.
> Everything which the fathers and mothers created I disown.
>
> (145)

And this rejection is likely to be violent:

> If I could throw a bomb and blow the whole neighborhood to
> smithereens I would do it. I would be happy seeing them fly in
> the air, mangled, shrieking, torn apart, annihilated.
>
> (226)

Miller's violence was reciprocal for the blood-sucking proclivities
of even his closest friends: everyman he regarded a potential
murderer, who insisted that he join the everyday club or have his

38 life snuffed out. For that reason Miller felt like a man who had been released from a lightless dungeon after years of incarceration: he had to be careful not to stumble and get run over (288). With well meaning enemies on every hand, he had to cling to the glimmer of life he felt faintly beating in his breast.

The syndrome, falseness, alienation, rejection, may be taken as a psychological disturbance infecting not only artists and writers but large segments of our society. It is at least that, but the attempt to account for it on a psychological basis alone leaves out of account the active power of what is "there," or what is taken to be "there." That is, it locates the ills of man in his inner self and fails to notice that the inner self, in the first instance, is shaped by the lived world. If the lived world is regarded as illusory or false, the self will react with alienation and rejection.

This notion of "world" is not easy to grasp. The Heideggerian shorthand in which the concept is often expressed does not make the matter less difficult. For example, in Heideggerian terms, the primordial world is the pre-eidetic totality of significations given with the ready-to-hand. But this formulation may be bypassed for a moment in favor of a less terse account by Theodore Roszak:

> Yet, even so, there lurks behind our socially certified morality some primordial world view which dictates what reality is, and what, within that reality, is to be held sacred.
>
> For most of us, this world view may elude the grasp of words; it may be something we never directly attend to. It may remain the purely subliminal sense of our condition that spontaneously forms our perceptions and our motivations. Even before our world view guides us to discriminate between good and evil, it disposes us to discriminate between real and unreal, true and false, meaningful and meaningless. Before we act in the world, we must conceive of a world; it must be *there* before us, a sensible pattern to which we adapt our conduct.
>
> (80)

The primordial world view to which Roszak refers is thus an order of things which the self finds already "there" upon its insertion into the world.

World in this sense is already there because it is pre-eidetic, i.e.

it is carried along with the cultural tradition as the preconceptual or subconceptual horizon of all dispositions to the real: we come upon the world we do because we learn to acknowledge the regnant though unspoken sense of things and their order. World is thus the totality of significations man inherits with his culture, principally his language. This world embraces all objects of the lived world because it is given with whatever is ready-to-hand — to continue the exposition of Heideggerian terms. That is, every object within the experienced world has the place and value it does because it belongs to the received order; nothing is or can be experienced that does not already belong to that order. It is thus possible to say that the totality of significations is given with every object one comes upon.

The world is there before we perceive it, think about it, act upon it. It is given with the symbol system of the culture, as its deep structure. It is that to which the self gives itself, and which, in turn, gives itself to the self.

In a literalminded age like our own, the world in which we presume to dwell is taken to be simply congruent with the real. The curse of literalmindedness, which in our case is grounded in a sophisticated empiricism, is that it conflates its own construction of reality with the real, and hence cannot allow for the stresses and strains of incongruity. The world bequeathed to literalminded man is like a concrete highway built without expansion joints: the freezes and thaws produced by the hot and cold draughts of the real are breaking it up. This highly figurative speech is a way of saying that artists and poets like Henry Miller intuit that the modern lived world is no less a construction than earlier worlds, but the naïve faith that it is the really real and no mistake will only bring the destruction of the self in its wake. For the self intuitively knows that it will never confront raw and eternal reality in its nakedness; it always encounters a construction which is in part of its own making. Not to recognize this truth is a deception of the most fundamental order.

If falseness and alienation constitute more than the passing fancies of demented souls — at least a half-dozen generations of

40   artists attest to the authenticity of such fancies — then we are driven to the conclusion that the received world is in some sense an illusion; it appears to be cracking up, in spite of our naïve faith, under the impact of some other reality. What is "there" turns out to be something quite different from what was taken to be there. What is there is pressing new claims, through the artist, on man, who tends to be a forgetful, insensitive, and arrogant partner in the constitution of the world.

Henry Miller and his ilk have been exiled from the received world and gone in mad search of a new world under the duress of a new reality: "I am the germ of a new insanity, a freak dressed in intelligible language, a sob that is buried like a splinter in the quick of the soul" (121). The artist is mad, or aspires to be mad, because the received world is what certifies the sanity of the everyday. He therefore takes out an insanity license in order to pass unmolested beyond the frontier of the immense solidity of the self-evident; he proposes to heed the call of the new reality by flying away on a moth-eaten magic carpet.

The psychological account of the artistic malady belongs to the teacher stage of the degeneration:

> Nothing is right or wrong but thinking makes it so.
> You no longer believe in reality but in thinking.

(63)

The protest on the part of Miller is a protest in part against the view that reality is vested in the categories of the mind. Such an inversion of what the literal mind takes to be the fact rests on the conflation of thought and reality: if there is no discrepancy between thought and reality that cannot be adjudicated by clearer thinking, then valid, i.e. literal, thought self-evidently reflects the real. Analytic philosophy was tempted, for a time, by this premise. But Miller, like many of his artistic contemporaries, is harassed by the conviction that he cannot by taking thought make one hair of his history white or black; that he cannot discern the contours of the real by rational analysis. He is thus driven to divest himself of the conceptual clutter that obscures the real, in order to allow the real to present itself to him.

The task he sets himself has herculean proportions just because it cannot be fulfilled by thought and is beyond the competence of the will. It is as though, given the circumspections indicated, he has no choice but to assault phenomena violently, with the whole of his being at issue, in the hope that he will somewhere, someplace, somehow bump up against a real object. He roots, hogs, and dies in the pig-pen of experience, in the effort to grub out a fragment of real sustenance, some contact with bedrock. He cannot get purchase on himself in an illusory world; he must have an anchor in the real.

> What strikes me now as the most wonderful proof of my fitness, or unfitness, for the times is the fact that nothing people were writing or talking about had any real interest for me. Only the object haunted me, the separate, detached, insignificant *thing*. It might be a part of the human body or a staircase in a vaudeville house; it might be a smokestack or a button I found in the gutter. Whatever it was it enabled me to open up, to surrender, to attach my signature.
>
> (54)

And it was to the quest for the isolated object, without benefit of conceptual guidance, that Miller devoted himself.

The quest for the real is linked, of course, to his passion to become a writer, to become an artist, to be able to speak with his own voice, as opposed to the voices of his forebearers and predecessors.

First of all, something to which he could attach his signature was the *sine qua non* of his being. It was the fundamental datum on which everything else depended. And because he could locate the real only in rare instances of ecstatic experience, he found it impossible to say what he thought or felt:

> Whether I die today or tomorrow is of no importance to me, never has been, but that today even, after years of effort, I cannot say what I think and feel — that bothers me, that rankles. From childhood on I can see myself on the trace of this specter, enjoying nothing, desiring nothing but this power, this ability. Everything else is a lie — everything I ever did or said which did not bear upon this. And that is pretty much the

42   greater part of my life.

(Tropic of Capricorn: 13f.)

That is essentially the confession of the two *Tropics*.

For Miller to be able to say what he thinks and feels he would have to know who he is, and to know who he is he would have to come into touch with the real. The achievement of the latter requires that he become an artist:

> I didn't dare to think of anything then [in his first book] except the "facts." To get beneath the facts I would have had to be an artist, and one doesn't become an artist overnight. First you have to be crushed, to have your conflicting points of view annihilated. You have to be wiped out as a human being in order to be born again as an individual . . .. One can't make a new heaven and earth with "facts." There are no "facts" — there is only *the fact* that man, every man everywhere in the world, is on his way to ordination.

(35)

And to become an artist means to be able to bring the real to expression, to embody it in language:

> I must have the ability and the patience to formulate what is not contained in the language of our time, for what is now intelligible is meaningless.

(122f.)

Since that is beyond him for the moment, he can only fall silent:

> I shall say nothing until the time comes again to be a man.

(123)

> For me the most excruciating agony was to have the word annihilated before it had even left my mouth. I learned, by bitter experience, to hold my tongue; I learned to sit in silence, and even smile, when actually I was foaming at the mouth. I learned to shake hands and say how do you do to all these innocent-looking fiends who were only waiting for me to sit down in order to suck my blood.

(288)

These last words sum it up: becoming an artist, bringing the new reality to expression is a high risk enterprise just because the agony of a fresh, underived word is rewarded with instant annihilation: the blood suckers would not permit such a word to escape.

The artist, nevertheless, is in quest of a new world, the really real world, which will allow him to become a man again and to bring that world into language. He cannot be sure he will find that world — he only believes it is there — but he is willing to risk his soul, i.e. his destiny, in the venture. Miller sums it up this way:

> I am going back to a world even smaller than the old Hellenic world, going back to a world which I can always touch with outstretched arms, the world of what I know and see and recognize from moment to moment. Any other world is meaningless to me, and alien and hostile. . . . What this world is like I do not know, nor am I even sure that I will find it, but it is my world and nothing else intrigues me.
>
> (146)

> Above all I was an eye, a huge searchlight which scoured far and wide, which revolved ceaselessly, pitilessly, ... If I longed for destruction it was merely that this eye might be extinguished.. . . I wanted that eye extinguished so that I might have a chance to know my own body, my own desires. I wanted to be alone for a thousand years in order to reflect on what I had seen and heard — *and in order to forget*. I wanted something of the earth which was not of man's doing, something absolutely divorced from the human of which I was surfeited. I wanted something purely terrestrial and absolutely divested of idea. I wanted to feel the blood running back into my veins, even at the cost of annihilation.
>
> (76)

Anything less than radical risk would be sure to fail.

For the priest reality is revealed. The real is assured and insured by the gods. The tradition is reliable. So understood, the priestly tradition has suffered decay. In the authentic priestly tradition, reality, even the gods, was understood metaphorically or non-literally; there could thus be a variety of explanations, even conflicting ones, for the same set of phenomena. In the tradition as decayed, however, the revealed reliable tradition is taken as literal.

44   For the teacher reality is rational. The real is vested in categories of the mind. Nothing is right or wrong but thinking makes it so. The tradition must submit to rational criticism, which in the end determines what is real/unreal, right/wrong.

To the artist of our time what is taken to be real is illusory; the common world is phony. The tradition merely deceives, reinforces the illusion, because it makes pretentious claims to ultimate truth. The artist forsakes the sanity of the received world and goes in mad search of the really real.

Updike's statement of the degeneration from priest to teacher to artist represents the historical breach reflected in Nietzsche, Kafka, Camus coming to ever clearer expression in the common consciousness. That historical breach is the disjunction between the received world and another, more real world. Henry Miller provides us with a paradigmatic case of the artist — the final term of Updike's trajectory — in search of the real. As the time of our time continues to arrive as something increasingly seen and heard, it will erupt — it has erupted — also in the religious sphere, perhaps crucially, since the initial term of the degeneration is the priest.

III

The declension, priest, teacher, artist, marks the move away from an ordinary, certified, comfortable reality toward a non-ordinary, less determined, surprising form of world. And in Updike's triad the final term is the artist, which lies at the far end of the trajectory from the priest.

In the revolutions of the 1960's, another final term appeared to emerge. While bearing many of the same marks as the artist, the new end term took on distinctly religious overtones. Theodore Roszak has noted the religiosity of Allen Ginsberg (124ff.), Tom Wolfe of the Kesey group (111-16), and don Juan in the writings of Carlos Castaneda is a man of knowledge or a *sorcerer*. It is possible that artist and holyman are two faces of the same phenomenon; it is also possible that Updike's triad has become a tetrad with the sorcerer or seer as the new final figure. In that case, perhaps the development has come full circle: from priest to priest — but on a new plane.

The man of knowledge to which Castaneda aspires and which don Juan embodies is a figure which speaks immediately to the thousands of mostly young who endeavored to take a "trip" or get "on the bus" during the past decade and more. Like them, Castaneda is on a "journey to Ixtlan," in quest of "a separate reality." Also like them, he begins his journey with the aid of drugs.

In *Journey to Ixtlan* (1972), Castaneda confesses that in the first two volumes (1968, 1971) he had misunderstood don Juan: he took don Juan to mean that the use of psychotropics was the only avenue to the perception of a new reality; actually, don Juan was teaching him the description of a non-ordinary reality, was helping him to "stop" the world and to "see." Once he acquired "membership" among those who knew the description of the new order of things, he no longer needed the help of drugs (see *Ixtlan*: 7-14).

Ken Kesey, too, proposed taking "the next step in the psychedelic revolution" (Wolfe: 339), the step beyond the use of LSD. But the "graduation" of the merry pranksters was premature: the time was not yet ripe for unaided "seeing." Nevertheless, Kesey had a vision of the step beyond.

The initial use of drugs was linked, in many manifestations of the movement, to altered sight. Drugs were necessary because of the stubbornness of the case or because old eyes were not up to the task. As Tom Wolfe puts it for the merry pranksters, "All of us have a great deal of our minds locked shut. We're shut off from our world" (39f.). Drugs are the necessary means of opening the doors of perception. Under the influence of drugs, one looks out through "completely strange eyeholes." Drugs are thus the means of renewing contact with the real world, of recovering one's birthright to see, a birthright of which one is robbed by the brain.

Castaneda also emphasizes that the description of the ordinary world is something learned as a child. Once learned, it is very tenacious indeed because it is assumed to be final. In order to be able to see the world differently, some powerful antidote is needed (*Ixtlan*: 13). Further, the real world is fleeting, according to don Juan, and only the "smoke" can provide the speed one needs to see it. One could perhaps learn to do it unaided, but the body could not stand the stress (*A Separate Reality*: 9, 112). With worlds tumbling over each other before man's very eyes, only the "smoke" can accelerate seeing sufficiently to bring these strange worlds into focus.

The case of Carlos Castaneda's apprenticeship to don Juan is perhaps not atypical of comparable movements: as preoccupation with drugs recedes, the real issues become clearer. And the real issues have to do with what is to be escaped as preparation for a journey to a place that can be defined only as away-from-here.

Like Henry Miller the artist, the sorcerer don Juan is persuaded that the common perception of the everyday world is only a description hammered into the child from the moment it is born. The child learns the description in conjunction with the onslaught of perception as such: the two become linked in his mind. As a consequence, the received world strikes the young perceiver as an endless flow of perceptions which fit the description. The congruity between the way the child perceives the world and the description taught him makes that child a member of a community (*Ixtlan*: 8f., 299).

Since the flow of perceptions conforms to the description, there is very little possibility that the flow will be broken by a perception that does not fit the description, i.e. one that is simply mysterious or one that calls for a different description. As the received description becomes habituated, the possibility of nonconformity becomes even more remote. In a literalminded age like our own, the illusion is created that the description which makes one a member of the community is simply and completely congruent with the real world itself: there can be no other description because there is no other world to describe. There are, perhaps, a few remaining mysteries to be fitted into the known description, but there is no other reality to which sight should be accommodated.

The fundamental premise of the sorcerer is that there are many descriptions of many realities (*Ixtlan*: 9). Among them, of course, is the common description. That one is least interesting, however, because it is the most restrictive and because it tends to exclude other descriptions. The question whether the common description was so restrictive in every age does not concern don Juan or Castaneda. In any case, the sorcerer's chief task is to break the stranglehold of the common description on his perceptions. The same point can be made metaphorically: the sorcerer must embark on a journey to Ixtlan (*Ixtlan*: 300) or away-from-here. They are the same place.

The world man commonly knows is reflexive: the world conforms to our description of it (*Tales*: 30). The everyday description of reality thus stands between us and our experience of world. In that case, what we actually experience is a recollection of our experience as filtered through the description (*Tales*: 53). Contact with reality must then be characterized as the memory of a contact (*Tales*: 54f.). For this reason, it is not surprising that don Juan characterizes sight as chained by reason (*A Separate Reality*: 260) and maintained by talking (*Tales*: 101). And habituated sight pulls the other senses in its train: a thunderous rumble is "seen" as an avalanche because Castaneda draws on a repertoire of accumulated audio associations he has derived largely from the cinema (*A Separate Reality*: 252f.).

Don Juan is not given to the rage against the tyranny of the received world so characteristic of Henry Miller. Nevertheless, the sorcerer is a warrior who must constantly be on guard against his enemies, one of which is clarity (*Teachings*: 80f.). The journey is a battle, but it is a battle concerned as much with the powers of the new reality as it is with the effort to free oneself from old tyrannies of sight and sound. Sometime between Miller and Castaneda the negative struggle was replaced by a confidence that a new reality

48   could, in fact, be reached.

For the man of knowledge the world is endless mystery (*A Separate Reality*: 219f.). The world is mystery because there are many worlds tumbling over one another before one's eyes (*Ixtlan*: 165; *A Separate Reality*: 154), or, one could also say, when one begins to "see" as a sorcerer, the world is fleeting, is in a constant state of flux (*A Separate Reality*: 9, 112). At that point, one no longer "knows" in the sense that one used to know; indeed, one no longer "knows" at all (194). "Knowledge" of the old order is not for the man of knowledge because the world is incomprehensible, something that he cannot "figure out." The world keeps its own initiatives, so to speak, in presenting itself to the sorcerer as now this, now that, and the sorcerer receives all impressions without weaving them into a logical whole or insisting that they "mean" something.

The sorcerer stands on the premise that there is more to the world than the average man sees. The average man tries to "figure out" what he sees and ends by making the world familiar, by making it conform to reason (*Ixtlan*: 167f.). He therefore domesticates what he sees, makes it fit the description. The world intended by the sorcerer, on the other hand, is the negation of what the everyday mentality takes as reality, i.e. is the world as perpetual mystery.

To apprehend the world as mystery is to become a sorcerer: the terms are synonymous. In his four-volume work, Castaneda approaches the matter of becoming a sorcerer both from the side of the teacher and from the side of the apprentice. The two can be conflated and reduced to one, since the descriptions tend to converge.

It is the task of the sorcerer to introduce the apprentice to the idea that his perception of the world is only a description which he learned, presumably as a child (*Tales*: 231). This is a very difficult task because perceptions are supported by a continual flow of interpretations that are taken to be part of the perceptions themselves. The flow of interpretations is part of the internal dialogue: the world is what it is to us and we are what we are because we keep telling ourselves that it is so (*Tales*: 40). The only way to get off the merry-go-round, which is a vicious circle (*Tales*: 100), is to stop the internal dialogue; by stopping the dialogue, we stop the world (the old one) (*Ixtlan*: 7-14, especially 14, 299).

Reason and talk are traps into which the perceiving person falls. Reason induces man to forget that the description he learned is only a description, and talk supports the blindness of reason (*Tales*: 100f.). For this reason, words are false friends. They make us think we are enlightened when we are not by giving us the description of things.

When the internal dialogue stops, we see inconceivable things, things which are normally kept heavily guarded by words (*Tales*: 40). Stopping the world thus has roughly the same effect as the "smoke," which also helped Castaneda to see things he could not fit into his description. Stopping the world frees the eyes to "see" (*Tales*: 172f.), and it is "seeing" that is the special goal of the sorcerer (*Ixtlan*: 14).

Don Juan makes it very clear that seeing is a very difficult thing to achieve. One cannot see merely by making a resolution to see or by wishing. Here the function of the teacher is critical: it is the teacher's job to give the apprentice a practical task, such as the right way of walking, which will claim his attention and divert it from the real issue (*Tales*: 231ff.). Diversion is essential because the reason must be tricked. If the reason is not lulled into thinking the old vision is safe, it will not release the eyes (*Tales*: 269). But if it can be persuaded that the self is not at stake, it will permit the old description to be shattered.

It is important to note that, in the teachings of don Juan, the shape of the self corresponds to the shape of the world that is perceived. In his final experience, Castaneda has the sensation of falling, spinning, exploding, disintegrating, until the self is no longer a unity in the old sense. It is a colony of selves, a colony, to be sure, which still understood the allegiance of one unit to another, but not a single awareness as in the old self (*Tales*: 269). The self becomes everything by becoming nothing (*A Separate Reality*: 153). This plurality of selves goes together with the

50   plurality of worlds perceived by that self.

The opposite side of the coin is that the old self, under the tutelage of don Juan, feels threatened: it cannot hold onto the old criteria for reality and hence begins to lose its self-assurance; when the old world is threatened, insantity is the inevitable sensation (*A Separate Reality*: 7, 262; *Tales*: 245).

Becoming a man of knowledge is not only disintegrating, it is also, fortunately, momentary (*Teachings*: 78). One becomes a man of knowledge in that moment when he glimpses the new reality. And what the man of knowledge learns in that vision is always unexpected; he never learns what he thinks he will learn (*Teachings*: 79). These two characteristics correspond to the fact that the new reality is fleeting (*A Separate Reality*: 9, 112) and that the new world is in constant flux.

The correlative of these features is that the self, which is inclined to think it is important (*A Separate Reality*: 81), loses its self-importance (*Ixtlan*: 37-45) when it can no longer give an account of what it perceives (*A Separate Reality*: 126). It also gives up the pretense of telling illusion from reality, although the new self is better positioned than the old self to do so (*Ixtlan*: 128). Indeed, the average man practices witchcraft, which may be defined as the practice of explaining everything by means of phony accounts (*A Separate Reality*: 127). The final test of the true man of knowledge is this: he must know that all explanations, all views of reality, including those of the sorcerer, are merely descriptions. There is no truth beyond the description.

The Parable of the Leaven:
Away-From-Here as the Destination

Biblical criticism is a species of literary criticism. If the range and function of literary criticism were clear, that remark would be more illuminating than it is. Yet in spite of the ambiguity of terms, the correlation is suggestive.

Literary criticism, on minimal terms, ought to instruct the uninitiated in what to read and how to read it. A guide to what is worthy of attention amidst the deluge of printed matter assaulting the optical nerves is alone worth the price of admission. Even after the sorting has been made, it may not be immediately evident to all why a particular piece merits close reading and reflection. All of which is to say, how a piece is to be read and whether it is worth reading in the first place are not unrelated questions.

The literary critic, according to George Steiner, has these two functions: his task is to "prepare the context of future recognition," and to widen and complicate the map of sensibility (8f.). The present reader is taught to see what is really there to be seen; failing the adequate transformation of present sensibility, the critic must lay the ground for delayed recognition. Criticism is

51

52   a second-order enterprise, but the poet could not survive without it.

The biblical corpus is large enough to warrant, even require, selective attention. And because it has suffered overattention, its language has been overlayed with tons of obfuscating debris. To change the metaphor, few literary compendia in the Western tradition have been so completely washed clean of resonances by the waters of common repetition and interpretation. Is it possible to restore some of those resonances or cart away some of that debris? If so, what is the appropriate critical methodology?

One thing may be stipulated by way of anticipation: the methodology must be appropriate to the subject matter.

I

Away-from-here: The Point of Departure

The first question that naturally arises in connection with the interpretation of any text is where does one begin? The student learning to do exegesis finds getting started the most difficult task of all. Once a start has been made, however, one is able, as a rule, to proceed to a conclusion without faltering.

There is point in the last remark: the way in which the task of interpretation is *undertaken* is determinative for the whole process. The *undertaking* anticipates what is to be *overtaken*. Methodology is not an indifferent net; it catches only what it is designed to catch. For this reason, phenomenology has been preoccupied with the methodology, but not as an enterprise independent of the subject matter. The slogan, "to the things themselves," suggests that the thing itself should be permitted to propose the terms of its unconcealment.

The matter may be left vague for the moment. To return to the initial question: where does one begin? The interpreter begins where he must. But where must he begin? *He must set out from where he is.* Where he is, of course, is his particular time and place in history in relation to the text under scrutiny.

The naïveté of this common-sense reply should not deceive. In the first place, it is no easy matter to determine precisely where one is. Writing the history of the last fifty years is always the most hazardous task. The future of these years has not yet fallen out into the sunlight of historical distance. In the second place, the advice presupposes that where one is in relation to the interpretation of a given text is in some sense (as yet undefined) a misinterpretation, a misunderstanding, or a nonunderstanding of that text. There would be no need for fresh interpretation were it not assumed that previous interpretation was in some respects deficient.

To put the difficulties concisely: one is to set out from where one is as a place that cannot be located with precision and move away from some unspecified misunderstanding or nonunderstanding in the direction of some unspecified understanding to a future that comports authentically with both the subject matter of the text one is interpreting and with the context in which the text is to be interpreted.

To mark the way to this elusive destination the map has not yet been drawn. When the knowledge requisite to the map is in hand, there will no longer be any need for the map. Meanwhile, only the direction of the quest is certain: it is away-from-here, away from established understanding which also entails misunderstanding and nonunderstanding.

The real gravity of the dilemma may now be discerned: how can the text propose the terms of its unconcealment when the terms themselves are dependent upon a glimpse of the text already unconcealed? *Mis*understanding and *non*understanding can give way to understanding only when the *mis* and the *non* are exposed by some understanding.

Getting underway, consequently, is of crucial importance. The appropriate analysis will proceed circumspectly; it will endeavor to coax the text into betraying its own intentionality by pressing the issue with the text, all the while looking for the stray clue dropped inadvertently along the path of violent wrestling with the

54   tradition.

It may prove lucrative to advance these preliminary abstractions as a down payment on the analysis of a concrete text. A biblical text that is relatively free of ambiguities is to be preferred; but, alas, such a text is not to be found. Since ambiguity and complexity characterize every text, brevity will have to supply the virtue. For reasons that will eventually emerge, the parable or similitude of the leaven, taken from the Jesus tradition, has been chosen for scrutiny.

The parable of the leaven is reported by Matthew and Luke in a form without significant variation: "The Kingdom of heaven is like leaven which a woman took and hid in three measures of meal, till it was all leavened" (Mt 13:33; cf. Lk 13:20f.). The parable is presumably derived from Q and is reported in both cases as a twin to the parable of the mustard seed.

The Gospel of Thomas preserves a slightly different version: "The kingdom of the father is like a woman, who has taken a little leaven and has hidden it in dough and has made large loaves of it" (Thomas 96). Most interpreters of Thomas hold that this version does not represent a significant alternative to the Synoptic tradition.

In accordance with sound scholarly practice, and as a means of locating approximately where the modern interpreter is, the history of recent interpretation may be briefly sampled. Joachim Jeremias, the oracle of modern parable interpretation, avers that the meaning of this parable, like that of the mustard seed, is that "out of the most insignificant beginnings, invisible to human eye, God creates his mighty Kingdom, which embraces all the peoples of the world" (149). For Jeremias the parable is a parable of contrast: the "tiny morsel of leaven" is "absurdly small in comparison with the great mass of more than a bushel of meal" (148). The parable is aimed at the doubts of those who hesitated to believe that the Kingdom of God could issue from the insignificant beginnings of Jesus' ministry. It is therefore a parable of assurance (149).

Jeremias interprets the leaven jointly with the mustard seed because, he says, the two are closely linked by content. He admits that their juxtaposition in Q may derive from a collector or redactor (146). One may wonder whether the compiler of Q has not in fact skewed the interpretation of one or both of the parables by placing them together. In any case, Jeremias appears to have determined that the connection is valid.

C. H. Dodd in a somewhat earlier work toys with the idea that the leaven should be interpreted without reference to the mustard seed. If taken independently, he claims, it means that Jesus' ministry is comparable to leaven working in dough: it works from within, without external coercion, "mightily permeating the dead lump of religious Judaism . . ." (155f.). If it goes with the mustard seed, then "the emphasis must lie upon the completion of the process of fermentation. The period of obscure development is over; . . . the Kingdom . . . has now come" (154). In either case, Dodd's thesis that the Kingdom is here and now present and effective is substantiated.

This sample of opinion may be augmented by notice of one other ranking scholar of parables.

Adolf Jülicher is the father of all recent parable interpretation. In his mammoth two-part work, pubished in 1899 and 1910, he not only reviews the history of interpretation but establishes the guidelines that parables are to be stripped of all allegorical overlay and interpreted in accordance with one point of the broadest possible (moral) application (Dodd: 24ff.; Jeremias: 18ff.). For Jülicher's one generalized moral, A. T. Cadoux, Dodd, and Jeremias propose to substitute one particular point of historical application, namely, the point that suits Jesus' historical setting. In other respects, however, they agree with Jülicher that the parables score a didactic point that can be readily reduced to more discursive language. Jülicher thus launched modern interpretation on its course, and the search for that one elusive point of particular historical application has gone on relentlessly, but largely without decisive resolution.

With the rejection of allegory, the details of the picture or narrative were reduced to incidental features of the parable.

56   Determine the point, it is said, and the details fall into place. But how is one to determine the point without first ascertaining what detail or which details are the vehicle of the point? According to Jeremias, the parable contrasts insignificant beginnings with great issue. The tiny morsel of leaven is thus contrasted with the huge mass of dough. How do we know that it is just these two details which convey the point, while the leaven and the dough themselves are incidental? Dodd, again, fastens on the process of fermentation as the clue to the point: like leaven working in dough, the Kingdom works in the world or in Judaism. Dodd has elected quite a different detail from which to adduce his point, and, one might suppose, with equal justification, since the process of selection appears to be arbitrary. Alternately, Dodd can fix on the leavened lump of dough as a sign of the Kingdom's arrival. In either case, he is following Jülicher's fundamental maxim: one point corresponding more or less to one detail of the narrative or picture. Jeremias, by contrast, often sneaks in two or more details in order to win his single point.

Dodd and Jeremias are struggling with Jülicher's legacy without realizing they have been trapped by it. Instead of recovering the parable by discarding allegory, they have been thrown into anarchy: choose a detail, any detail, and draw the point. The point drawn is as reliable as the choice of detail, or as reliable as the theology informing the point that prompts the choice of detail.

Jülicher's legacy is a trap because he was never able to escape from the allegory he so fervently rejected. For him and his successors parable interpretation is a form of reduced allegory; instead of many points corresponding to a variety of details, there is only one point corresponding to one, or a pair of details.

Parable interpretation is at an impasse. The way forward is away-from-here.

II

Away-from there:
Sedimented and Refracted Language

The ultimate point of departure in addressing a text is away-from-here, as the interpreter's locus within the history of interpretation. The penultimate point of departure is away-from-there, as the writer or speaker's locus within his own linguistic tradition. The former has already been addressed. Attention may now be given to the justification and exposition of the latter.

As a tradition matures, its myths, symbols and lexical stock, its semantic logic, are crystallized. The meanings evoked by the terms of a culture are sedimented. The crystallization and sedimentation of a tradition constitute the immediate background within which and against which one speaks or writes the language. If one merely traffics in the sedimented tradition, one merely repeats what is already contained in the language. Under these circumstances, the text produced is rightly interpreted within the framework of the sedimented or dictionary meanings of the terms.

The dictionary represents a tacit social compact to which every speaker must subscribe if he wishes to speak intelligibly. Yet even the poorest speaker or writer, because he has learned to manipulate a finite system of grammatical and semantic variables, so as to be able to produce, potentially, an infinite string of novel sentences, never simply repeats what is already contained in the language. As a matter of fact, the semiliterate and illiterate constantly produce novel sentences in daily parlance that infringe the established grammatical and semantic conventions. Only the fully literate has any real prospect of trading in fully sedimented speech because only he is sufficiently familiar with the conventions to be able to rehearse them.

This point should be kept in mind as a rejoinder to those who hold that Jesus trafficked in the sedimented language of late

Judaism *because he was unliterary.*

There is another reason sedimented speech is essentially unstable. A pure recapitulation of the tradition is a task of herculean, if not divine, proportions, as any good historian can attest. History does not pause sufficiently long to allow one to repeat even the same string of linguistic symbols without the temporal passage taking its modifying toll. What is said in one moment is modified when reiterated in the next by the same speaker just because the "I" of the speaker has shifted its temporal locus.

The unrepeatability of the tradition is a limiting concept of no little significance, but it is not the immediate issue.

The creative writer, in contrast to the hack or gossip, employs language as a means of refracting language. If he aspires to say something new, he must seek some exit from the vicious circle of sedimented meaning, and this exit is provided for by a deformation of the tradition. He cannot begin with new language. He must begin with the habituated language at hand, with the language he learned at his mother's knee. But he may succeed in moving away from those sedimentations and finding his own voice. The measure of his success is commensurate with the degree to which he has infringed the semantic compact represented by the dictionary.

Away-from-there as the penultimate point of departure means, consequently, that the interpreter must work out of the sedimented tradition as received by the author of a given text, and into the refraction or deformation of that tradition, as the author in question brings the tradition to speech afresh.

From this distance the parable of the leaven looks flat. It does not strike one as poignant; in fact, it probably does not strike the modern reader at all. One may conclude that the parable is trite and let it go at that. It is just possible that modern sensitivities have gone dead — a possibility one is initially inclined to regard as remote since the parable has been domesticated in the language tradition. As historians one may nevertheless persist and indulge in a course of sensitivity training.

Two procedures are immediately open. First, one may bury oneself in the primary literature, read parables of all kinds, read texts on leaven, baking, and the like, and even read texts that have no apparent connection with the subject matter of this parable. The object will be to reacclimate oneself to the sedimented tradition of that time and place, with a view to "listening in" on the lost resonances of our text. Secondly, one may scan the secondary literature for items which show up, "appear," but do not converge with the interpreter's view of the parable. Such items may prove to be important as clues to both away-from-here and away-from-there on the grounds that they have not been assimilated to what the parable is taken to mean. Ideally, one should combine the two procedures.

Consider the parable sentence once again: "The kingdom is like leaven which a woman took and hid in three measures of meal until all was leavened." What items in the sentence stand out against the background of language sedimented "there"? Which items attract attention "here"? Which items show up as residual problems in the history of interpretation?

The scene is common enough. Anyone who has observed bread made, here or in the Near East, recognizes the scene for what it is: a piece of everydayness.

Well then, what clues are there beyond an undifferentiated common picture of a woman kneading dough for bread?

1. Even to the English reader the word "hid" may sound odd in the context of putting yeast into dough. In what sense does she "hide" the leaven? Jülicher is of the opinion that "hide" may have struck Matthew as appropriate to the situation of the Kingdom in the world at the time he wrote: it is hidden to the eyes of most men. However, Jülicher goes on to say that *kruptō* may also have been employed in a completely faded sense, meaning merely to *put* or *place in*. But the evidence he cites is slender (578). The word normally conveyed the nuance of *conceal, secret, cover*. Other

60   scholars avoid the question by averring that leaven is hidden in dough in the sense of disappearing in it, of becoming one with the dough it leavens. Dodd proposes that leaven is hidden in that, at first, nothing appears to happen (192); it is there, no longer with its own identity, but without apparent effect. This view is perhaps supported by the final phrase: "until the whole was leavened."

We hear elsewhere in the language of Jesus of things pertaining to the Kingdom being "hidden": the Father has *hidden* things from the wise and understanding (Mt 11:25; Lk 10:21); the Kingdom is likened to a treasure *hidden* in a field (Mt 13:44); indeed the mystery of the Kingdom is hidden in the parables themselves (cf. Mk 4:11f.). If hiddenness belongs to the essence of the Kingdom, as Günther Bornkamm maintains (71ff.), it is not surprising that the suggestion turns up in various contexts. In this case, the reader may have to do with a word deliberately chosen so as to vibrate in its context and thus attract attention, obliquely because metaphorically, to some horizon of the subject matter.

2. Although lost on the reader of the English translation, the unusual amount of meal involved in "three measures" would not have been lost on the original audience. The exaggerated amount has been a constant irritant to modern scholarship, especially to those who wish to affirm the everyday realism of the parables.

The precise value of the *saton* (Hebrew, *seah*) translated "measure," is not known. It may have amounted to as much as one and one-half pecks, or as little as two-tenths of a bushel (*IDB* IV: 834f.). The total amount may then have been slightly more than a half-bushel, or slightly more than a full bushel. Jeremias estimates three *seah* as about fifty pounds of flour, or enough to make bread for more than a hundred persons (147, and n. 7). In any case, we have to do with a "party" baking, as C. W. F. Smith puts it (72), or with preparations for a festive occasion of significant proportions.

Jeremias takes advantage of the large amount of dough in contrasting it with the "tiny morsel of leaven," yet he suggests that the number "three" may be an eschatological touch added by Matthew and Luke (147; more exactly, the redactor of Q?).

Support for the omission is afforded by the Gospel of Thomas, where the amount of meal is not specified. Perhaps the strongest argument for regarding the number as a gloss is that it constitutes a parallel to the "tree" in the mustard seed, which is almost certainly a modification of an original "shrub" or "bush," under the influence of the figure of the towering cedar in Ezekiel 17, 31 and Daniel 4.

These arguments are not without force. Nevertheless, there are even better reasons for retaining "three measures" as part of the original parable. These may be stated succinctly.

In the mustard seed, the smallness of the seed is emphasized, but not the size of the mature tree. The mustard plant constitutes a burlesque of the mighty cedar of Lebanon, a symbol for the mighty kingdoms of the earth. If the leaven were precisely parallel, we would expect the smallness of the leaven to be emphasized. But that is not in fact the case. "Leaven" is not qualified at all. What is qualified is the unusual amount of dough, and this comports well with Jesus' tendency elsewhere to indulge in comic exaggeration (e.g., hiring laborers at the eleventh hour, the celebration for the lost son, the size of the forgiven debt). That is to say, the parable of the leaven is devoid of comic exaggeration if the amount of flour is a secondary expansion.

Jeremias' suspicions were raised initially in this connection because of an Old Testament parallel. In Genesis 18, Yahweh visits Abraham by the oaks of Mamre in the form of three men. Abraham wishes to entertain his visitors with a "morsel of bread" on the occasion of this epiphany. He instructs Sarah to knead "three measures of fine meal" and from it to make cakes (Gen 18:6). A three-measure baking is thus suitable as an offering for an epiphany.

Gideon's experience at the oak of Ophrah parallels Abraham's at the oaks of Mamre /1/. Gideon prepares a kid (Abraham, a calf, Gen 18:7) and unleavened cakes from an ephah of flour (Judg 6:19). An ephah is comprised of three *seim* or three measures. Again, the amount is suitable for the celebration of an epiphany.

It may also be noted in passing that when Hannah dedicates

62   Samuel at the house of the Lord at Shiloh, she offers, among other things, an ephah or three measures of flour (1 Sam 1:24).

The everyday realism of the parable of the leaven appears to be shattered, then, on the gross amount of dough — about as much as a woman could knead at one time (Jülicher: 577), — and the specific amount is intended to suggest that the occasion is no ordinary one, perhaps even an epiphany (cf. Jeremias: 147).

3. It has been remarked that three measures of meal is associated with the epiphany or with a thank-offering to the Lord. If this overtone is taken as a clue to the horizon of the parable, one is brought back abruptly to the curious choice of the central figure of the parable. In this connection, two texts may be recalled:

> And you shall observe the feast of unleavened bread, for on this very day I brought your hosts out of the land of Egypt . . . For seven days no leaven shall be found in your houses; for if any one eats what is leavened, that person shall be cut off from the congregation of Israel, ...
>
> (Ex 12:17-20)

This injunction was joined by a more general injunction to the effect that leaven was prohibited in connection with sacrifices and meal offerings (Ex 23:18, 34:25; Lev 2:11, 6:17).

The second text reflects the annotations the symbol of leaven conjured up in the New Testament period (1 Cor 5:6-8). Leaven was apparently universally regarded as a symbol of corruption /2/. So pervasive was this understanding of leaven, in fact, that a number of commentators have remarked of the parable of the leaven: "an unexpected application of a familiar illustration" (122f.).

The difficulty of taking a figure predominantly associated with the "infectious power of evil" in a positive sense has often enough been observed by modern interpreters. C. W. F. Smith insists that leaven cannot be reinterpreted in a positive sense, given the sedimented understanding of the figure. And for Jesus to refract the sedimented understanding of the term in his own disposition to the Kingdom, would be to expect too much of Jesus' hearers

(71)! To this assertion must be responded: did Jesus allow his understanding of the Kingdom to be determined by the received tradition regarding the Kingdom?

But Smith and others are unaware of the real difficulty attached to reading the leaven in a positive sense because they have taken only perfunctory note of the sacramental overtones of the three measures of flour. Only Ernst Lohmeyer has grasped the real tension inherent in the juxtaposition. For Lohmeyer the inseparable connection between unleaven and the holy was so intense that the parable of the leaven could be understood only as part of an attack on temple and cult, an attack that comports with Jesus' displacement of the righteous and pious in Israel with the poor and destitute, the tax collectors and harlots: . . . "the tax collectors and prostitutes go into the kingdom, but you (the Pharisees) do not" (Mt 21:31) (220f.). Such an attack represents an inversion of the symbol of the unleavened and thus a refraction of the sedimented language tradition: the Kingdom arrives as a negation of the established temple and cult and replaces them with a sacrament of its own — a new and leavened bread.

It is just possible that his horizon is preserved less obliquely in the version in Thomas, where the woman makes large loaves (leavened?) out of the dough.

The proximity of the three terms, "leaven," "hide," "three measures of meal," within the confines of the brief sentence that comprises the parable, thus reverberate against each other and against the sedimented language tradition in such a way that the parable as a whole becomes plurisignificative. The terms are so subtly arranged that the unwary may well read it as a commonplace illustration of a commonplace bit of wisdom. But for the alert the parable triggers the imagination: the terms and the whole are set free to play against one another and against the tradition. Those who have ears hear strange voices.

III

Mode and Meaning

Listening in on the language opens the way for a consideration of mode and meaning. The words and sentences, when allowed to have their own say — against preconceived notions of what they mean — put one on the track of the subject matter, so to speak. But the subject matter is not something else, to be divorced entirely from the words. *What* the parable says cannot be simply divorced from the *way* it says. Form and content are wedded.

The Kingdom may be compared to: leaven which a woman took and hid in three measures of meal, until all was leavened. The leaven suggests an inversion of the locus of the sacred: there unleavened; in the Kingdom, leavened. *Hidden* hints that the presence of the Kingdom is not overtly discernible. Three measures of meal points to the sacramental power of the Kingdom, to the festive occasion of an epiphany. Over against the religious tradition into which Jesus was speaking, the Kingdom arrives as an inversion, as a mystery, and as power.

If the subject matter is characterized as mystery, then the mode of communication, if it is to be faithful to the subject matter, must convey that mystery as mystery. It may be put more strongly: the proclamation of the Kingdom cannot very well dispel the hiddenness without at the same time eroding the essence of the Kingdom. The mode of communication must be commensurate with the thing to be communicated.

The Kingdom *is* hidden. It does not arrive with observable signs, so that people can say, "Lo, here it is! or There! for behold . . . (Lk 17:21). And the Kingdom is proclaimed in parables, riddles, and dark sayings so that hearing, people hear not, and seeing, they see not (cf. Mk 4:12).

Furthermore, if the Kingdom comes as an inversion of what everybody takes to be the case with the sacred, then the terms of its proclamation will of necessity represent a refraction of sacred tradition. The last shall be first and the first last; the tax collectors and harlots go into the Kingdom but the righteous Pharisees do not. The mighty cedar becomes a lowly mustard shrub, the long-awaited Messiah arrives incognito. The unleavened is leavened; the holy becomes profane and the profane, holy. In sum, the Kingdom inverts the terms of the sacred and the profane.

If the mode and meaning of Jesus' language converge in both inversion and mystery, it may be anticipated that they will converge in power also. It is this convergence that has given rise to all the talk about language event. The conjunction of mode and meaning in power may be put concisely and provisionally this way: in the parables of Jesus the Kingdom is offered only for what it is, namely, a venture of faith undertaken on the authority of the parable, in the power of the parable. The parable authorizes the Kingdom into which it invites the hearer, and it empowers the hearer to cross over into that fabulous yonder.

IV

World-loss and World-gain

What does the parable authorize? In traditional language but with deliberate ambiguity, it can be said that the parable authorizes the arrival of the Kingdom of God. More precisely, the parable announces a Kingdom that is on its way, much as the imperial messenger in Kafka's parable is on its way (*Parables and Paradoxes*: 13ff.). For Kafka, the imperial messenger never arrives; in Jesus he has arrived, but his person and message lack the court credentials for which everyone looks. The Kingdom is therefore heralded by a messenger and in a mode that are unaccredited, or accredited only on their own authority.

Messenger, mode, and message, consequently, are conjoined. If one is prepared to perceive the arrival of the one, he is prepared to perceive all three. For this reason, it would be quite possible to speak of the Kingdom authorized by the parable in terms of any

66   one of its aspects. However, the message may be singled out here as the focal point.

Günther Bornkamm, in the work already cited, gives this interesting summary of the message: "To make the reality of God present: this is the essential mystery of Jesus. This making-present of the reality of God signifies the end of the world in which it takes place" (62). Observe three features of this summary: (1) Jesus makes the reality of God present; (2) this making-present is a mystery; (3) the presence of God, or the arrival of the Kingdom, brings an end to the world in which it arrives. Attention shall be focused on the last, but in so doing, something shall be noted about the first two as well.

In what sense does the Kingdom's arrival bring an end to the world in which it arrives? It is customary to think of the apocalyptic pictures drawn so fancifully by Daniel, Revelation, and the little apocalypse in the Synoptic Gospels. It is probably not possible for the modern interpreter to understand the apocalyptic mode in anything like its original sense. However, the language of Jesus directs attention to a different dimension of the question and provides fresh perspective on the problem.

What was the world into which Jesus came? To say that it was a world of sticks and stones, like one's own, is accurate but not very revealing. It is more illuminating to observe what lived world dominated the scene; to inquire after the way in which the Jews of Jesus' time and place experienced reality; to ask what referential nexus constituted the horizon of all possible experience, including the experience of God's reign.

In posing the question in this form, we are posing a phenomenological question. When Husserl stated that the world is "always already there," he meant that no one experiences an object without at the same time experiencing the horizon within which the object is located; the object is the focal point of a backlying referential nexus to which it belongs as object. As Ray Hart has put it, it is the shift in horizons that prompts one to "perceive a cow as so many pounds of beef rather than as something to be worshipped" (1970). But Husserl also meant that the perceiving consciousness is also "historically constituted: what is there is there in part as the history of consciousness has programmed it to apprehend" (Hart, 1970). The term "world," in a phenomenological sense, refers to the fundamental horizon or referential nexus within which consciousness apprehends and things are apprehended.

The religious world into which Jesus came — to limit consideration to one aspect of that world — was a world dominated by the law and the traditions of the fathers. The received world of Judaism in late antiquity was programmed to guard the deposit of tradition once for all delivered to Moses and the prophets, and to preserve this tradition against the day when Yahweh would restore his people to their rightful place within the economy of world history. In the meantime, Yahweh was taken to have withdrawn into the confines of sacred scripture and its interpretation by the fathers, into the temple and its cultus, into its latter day surrogate, the synagogue, and into those customs which overtly set the people of God off from their fellows. Within these confines Israel was to await, by faithful and patient observance of the law, the renewal of the ancient glory, to come, it was widely anticipated, in the near future.

It was into this world that Jesus burst with his herculean wrecking bar. His message can only be understood as something designed to precipitate the loss of the received world of Judaism in favor of the gain of the world of the Kingdom. The world in which the scribes and Pharisees were at home was shattered upon a new world designed for the poor and destitute, the tax collectors and sinners. The righteousness of the Pharisees was devalued as confederate paper. The temple and cultus were swallowed up in new forms of celebration: eating, drinking, and dancing in profane style. Sacred scripture was either ignored or criticized, and the traditions of the fathers were set down as millstones about the neck. In short, the home world of Judaism was turned upside down in the face of the new reality of the Kingdom.

The trauma produced by Jesus' message for those whose home world was Judaism is difficult to exaggerate; the hostility of the

68 scribes and Pharisees, for whom the loss of this world was nothing short of apocalyptic, is readily appreciated. On the other hand, the joy of the religiously disinherited, the destitute, the maimed and the blind was spontaneous. They had been invited to inhabit a strange, new, and alien world that demanded only that they celebrate its arrival as redemption from the past and openness to the future.

Meanwhile, the world of sticks and stones had not vanished in a cloud of apocalyptic smoke. To those who participated in the Kingdom, however, the world took a new shape, its objects hung together in a new way, and the things themselves were transformed as by a miracle. Reality itself underwent a metamorphosis. To those who refused this new reality, the world was very much the same, though perhaps less secure. These looked in vain to see what Jesus saw; what all the shouting was about they took to be senseless mystery — and from their point of view, rightly so.

In the message of Jesus, the loss of received world, the mystery of the Kingdom, and the making-present of the reality of God are coincident. In the parable of the leaven the coincidence is marked by the juxtaposition of "leaven" (loss of received world), "hide" (mystery), and "three measures of meal" (the presence of God). The parable thus parsimoniously encapsulates the horizons of the message of Jesus. World-gain is made concrete, is particularized, "instantiated" by the parable, as a passage for all who care to follow him.

V

Resedimentation: Handing the Tradition Around and On

According to B. T. D. Smith, the parable of the leaven probably owes its preservation to the fact that Christians saw in it a prophecy of the spread of the gospel and the extension of the church (123). The parable is not provided with a generalizing conclusion, as is the case with a number of other parables, so that one must infer how the later church understood it from some other premise. If the leaven was joined in the mustard seed subsequent to Jesus, there is basis for the inference that the metaphorical overtones of the parable were soon lost and its meaning reduced to an illustration of the infectiousness of the Kingdom. By the time of Ignatius, the figure of the leaven appears to have stood for the contrast between Judaism and Christianity. In his letter to the Magnesians, he writes: "Put aside then the evil leaven, which has grown old and sour, and turn to the new leaven, which is Jesus Christ. Be salted in him, that none among you may be corrupted, since by your savor you shall be tested. It is monstrous to talk of Jesus Christ and to practice Judaism" (Ign Mag 10.2f.). In this case, the fuller range of overtones, the plurisignificative character of the parable, has been lost, but the interpretation has preserved in ossified form the original constrast between the new faith and Judaism.

In the case of the mustard seed, we may observe how the burlesque of the mighty cedar of Israel in the original parable had faded, and the mustard plant converted back into a tree. This conversion may have been accompanied by additional emphasis on the smallness of the seed, as many interpreters, including Jeremias, believe. The mustard seed thus became at the hands of the church a parable of contrast, contrary to the opinion of Jeremias, who attributes this meaning to Jesus. In any case, the church "reinstitutionalized" the mustard plant, just as Ignatius "reinstitutionalizes" the leaven. "Institutionalizing" in this context means that the trauma of world-loss and world-gain has receded, and world, albeit in a new sense, is once again taken for granted.

It is inevitable that world-gain be freshly institutionalized or sedimented as it becomes established as tradition. In phenomenological parlance, tradition houses "received world," the circumspective horizon of all interpretation.

The emergence of world-gain is concomitant with what Ernst Fuchs calls language-gain. That is to say, new language is generated at the threshold of any new world as the means of access to and habitation in that world. Such foundational language, as it may be termed, grants the rights of passage, but it also tends to linger on in sedimented form to become the instrument of eviction. The rights of passage must perpetually be renewed at the price of a recovery of foundational language or the creation of yet another new language.

The sedimentation of foundational language has as its antidote one or more modes of secondary discourse, the function of which is to cast sedimentations, or tradition, back upon primary language and the experience of world-gain concomitant therewith. Failing appropriate modes of secondary language, primary or foundational language withers away in the dungeon of sedimented meanings until its pristine power is completely eroded by the vicious winds of common parlance. There is another possibility however: foundational language may die a historical death, given a radical shift in sensibility, in spite of all appropriate efforts to recover its horizon.

Foundational language is never totally lost to view within the continuity of a tradition. If the original language of a tradition has been forgotten, then the continuity of the tradition has been broken. The memory of an original tongue may grow extremely weak, as though its call were like the pealing of a distant bell. But the sedimentations will preserve that memory, though perhaps in a petrified form. It is for this reason that secondary analysis, like that undertaken in exegesis, may rediscover the wave length of foundational language, as it were, by "listening in" on that language and its sedimentations, as though from a great distance. In stumbling around for clues in the texts of the Jesus tradition and the history of interpretation, the interpreter is endeavoring to locate the trajectory of the original language by attending to the ways in which that language has "fallen out" in its subsequent history. Once on the right wave length, he may hope to recover something of its original horizon.

As the parables were sedimented in the Jesus tradition, their potential as parables was stopped down. The potential of the parable to evoke a fresh circumspective apprehension of the totality of what is there — a new world — was reduced to a specified meaning, a point, a teaching. This meaning or teaching could then be attached to the parable as a generalizing conclusion or be divorced from the parable and transmitted as a "truth." The point drawn from the parable diverts attention from the parable itself to what it teaches, and thus from the world onto which the parable opens to an idea in an ideological constellation, or, as we might also say, in a theology.

The loss of the parable as parable means the loss also of the cardinal points on the horizon onto which the parable originally opened. The inversion is lost and is replaced by contrast: it is no longer a matter of passage from world-loss to world-gain, but of the contrast between one world (e.g., pagan, Jewish) and another (Christian). The mystery is decoded as teaching or truth. And the making-present of the reality of God is exchanged for belief in God. Conversely, the recovery of the parable as parable restores the original horizon, namely, the inversion, the mystery, and the power.

The fundamental question for the interpreter who addresses himself to the Jesus tradition today is this: is it possible any longer to recover the parable as parable? Or has their been such a radical shift in world-gain? The answer depends upon whether the foundational language of Jesus is any longer living tradition.

VI

Technical and Essential Literacy

The analysis has come full circle. If the circuit has not been shorted, the return to the starting point will have occurred in another plane, and the circle will have become a spiral. Even so, success may not be imminent: an analysis of this type may turn out to be just one more opinion in the pantheon of opinions, unless or until it throws the interpreter back upon the text and leaves him there in solitude to confront the text without benefit of conceptual comforts.

72   Whether the parable of the leaven, or any part of the Jesus tradition, is living tradition cannot be answered in advance. The line between the life and death of symbols is too fine for certainty. A death certificate may make demise legal, but it does not make it irreversible.

Such metaphors, if resonant, suggest that the Jesus tradition has taken on the apprearance of death. What George Steiner says of the classics can be said also of the Christian tradition: it is not possible to edit classical texts or write commentaries on Scripture within a few kilometers of Buchenwald without some premonition that these languages no longer speak (54). Steiner puts it in another way: "He who has read Kafka's *Metamorphosis* and can look into his mirror unflinching may technically be able to read print, but is illiterate in the only sense that matters" (11). It is a live question whether proverbial modern man, within or without the church, is any longer literate in the only sense that matters with respect to the foundational language of the Christian faith.

Appropriate criticism can teach one to read texts with larger eyes, but it cannot make literate. The text alone has that power. Biblical criticism, like the literary criticism, comes anon to the end of its way: from that point he who aspires to literacy must go on alone.

/1/   The tree as the locus of divine epiphany in these accounts is faintly suggestive of the juxtaposition of the mustard (tree) and leaven in the synoptic tradition, but the concatenation is, I think, merely fortuitous. The mustard is linked with the mighty cedar rather than the oak.

/2/   Even among the Greeks, to judge by Plutarch and Persius (*IDB* III: 105).

Jesus as Magician

The Magic Beyond Truth (John Fowles)

The Magic Beyond Truth

I

Consider this sequence from the opening pages of John Fowles'
novel, *The Magus*:

> . . . I went to Oxford; and there I began to discover I was not
> the person I wanted to be.
>
> I had long before made the discovery that I lacked the
> parents and ancestors I needed.

(11)

Upon quitting his teaching post at the end of one year:

> It poured with rain the day I left. But I was filled with
> excitement, a strange exuberant sense of taking wing. I didn't
> know where I was going, but I knew what I needed. I needed a
> new land, a new race, a new language; and, although I couldn't
> have put it into words then, I needed a new mystery.

(15)

Then, later, astride Mt. Hymettus, looking down on Athens
and its seaport, Piraeus, out to a transparent sea the hue of a
mountain lake, with islands sprinkled here and there, and away to

76   the mountainous serenity of the Peloponnesus, he pauses, breathless from the climb and his fresh arrival in Greece:

> It was like a journey into space. I was standing on Mars, knee-deep in thyme, under a sky that seemed never to have known dust or cloud. I looked down at my pale London hands. Even they seemed changed, nauseatingly alien, things I should long ago have disowned.
>
> (45)

Here, in a few provocative strikes, Fowles sketches the essential contours of his tale: the wrong ancestors and nauseatingly alien hands; an expectant venture into new space; the anticipation of a new language and a new mystery. These contours are by now familiar; they constitute a paradigm of the artist-rebel of the period.

Nicolas Urfe, the principal in *The Magus* and the narrator of the story, was born in 1927 of middle-class parents "in the grotesquely elongated shadow . . . of that monstrous dwarf Queen Victoria" (11). The year 1927 epitomizes that wave of optimistic humanity washed up on the shores of middle-class mentality and mores between the First and Second World Wars. The mentality and mores of that shore were an alluvial deposit of the Victorian age. Thus, the members of that generation — those a bit over thirty but not yet at retirement — came to a home that was not their own, programmed to follow a script, the setting and dialogue for which were borrowed from a Victorian drawing room.

A premonition of the artificiality of that scene lurks in the mental recesses of all who belong to that generation. Parents and ancestors seem grossly inappropriate. And pale London hands strike the possessor as faintly disgusting. Disillusionment, alienation, and rejection are never far away; there is the constant temptation to quit one's home, relatives, and race.

The need of different ancestors, of a new land and a new race, is joined by Fowles to the need of a new language. The need is felt, initially, as privation. Says Urfe:

> Words had lost their power, either for good or for evil; still
> hung, like a mist, over the reality of action, distorting,
> misleading, castrating; but at least since Hitler and Hiroshima
> they were seen to be a mist, a flimsy superstructure.
>
> (185)

Yet, precisely in the privation, in the loss of language, is the
restrictive, confining power of language felt most intensely: dead
and lifeless words hang like a shroud over reality; they deceive and
distort; they rob manhood of imaginative potency.

Nicolas Urfe was bound in servitude to and by the old tongue,
his ancestral dialect. So long as he did not look through and
beyond the words, his confinement was solitary, lightless,
waterless. But once the intuition arises that language is not a wall
but a window, speech becomes an indifferent, even a permissive,
warden. For Urfe, the powerful but unseen presence of a new
reality began to crack the immense solidity of the old unreality.
Which is to say that his keeper, language, was not really
constructed to block out the light, any more than a sieve is made to
contain water. With emanations striking him from all sides, Urfe
became aware of the curious paradox.

> There was no word, it arrived, descended, penetrated from
> outside. It was not an immanent state, it was a conferred state, a
> presented state. I was a recipient. But once again there came
> this strange surprise that the emitters stood all around me I
> was having feelings that no language based on concrete
> physical objects, on actual feeling, can describe. I think I was
> aware of the metaphoricality of what I felt. I knew words were
> like chains, they held me back; and like walls with holes in
> them. Reality kept rushing through; and yet I could not get out
> to fully exist in it.
>
> (225f.)

The chains of the old tongue burst asunder; reality came rushing
through the fissures in the tradition; he felt proximity to a new
language, and hence a new reality.

It also occurred to Nicolas Urfe, as he glanced back over his
shoulder at Oxford and England, that he needed a new mystery.
The one bequeathed him had apparently been profaned. In Greece

78   he hoped to discover a new mystery, or perhaps recover an old one. Curiously enough, when he did stumble upon it, it drew near in the form of a parable, a fairy tale, the text of which he found in a cave (499f.).

The tale tells of a young prince who did not believe in princesses, in islands, or in God, because his father, the king, told him that such things did not exist. One day the prince ran away and came to another land. There, from the shore, he saw islands, and on the islands strange and troubling creatures. A man in evening dress approached the prince and confirmed his suspicions: those were real islands and real princesses. The stranger announced that he himself was God.

The prince returned home and reproached his father with his newly acquired truth. The king asked him how the man who claimed to be God was dressed. The prince replied that the man wore full evening dress, and that the sleeves of his coat were rolled back. The king smiled. "That," he said, "is the uniform of a magician."

The prince hurried back to the strange shore. When the man in tails appeared, the prince confronted him: "You deceived me last time, because you are a magician. But now I know the truth." The man smiled and said: "In your father's kingdom are many islands and princesses. But you are under his spell and so cannot see them."

Back in the palace, the young prince found his father and looked him in the eye:

"Father, is it true that you are not a real king, but only a magician?"

The king smiled and rolled back his sleeves.

"Yes, my son, I am only a magician."

"Then the man on the shore was God."

"The man on the shore was another magician."

"I must know the real truth, the truth beyond magic."

"There is no truth beyond magic," said the king.

The intricate maze of appearances Maurice Conchis had laid for Nicolas Urfe that summer on the island of Phraxos was intended to front him with one truth: there is no truth beyond magic. Urfe, true to the mindset of his age, stubbornly refused the lesson. Instead, he insisted on reading the drama as a detective story, one containing a mystery that could be solved, resolved, profaned, by digging out the facts, driving behind appearances, ripping off masks. Though he had intimations of the inviolate mystery, his eyes, ears, and tongue would not let him forsake the demeanor of Sherlock Holmes (cf. 501).

John Fowles has so constructed *The Magus* that the reader, like the protagonist, is lured down that broad, familiar road to self-deception and utter frustration. Both insist on the truth beyond magic. Only in retrospect, in the distance of reflection, will it dawn on the reader that he missed the crucial turn, tricked by his own proclivities, in concert with Nicolas Urfe. Only then will it occur to him that the truth beyond magic is — more magic.

II

It is a source of constant bewilderment and frustration that Jesus had so little to say by way of explicit direction for getting on in the world. He did of course leave perfectly lucid injunctions like "love your enemies," and "give to everyone who begs of you." But anyone who has faced the draft or walked the streets of a major city knows how unrealistic these maxims are. Some of his teachings are comfortable because they no longer apply or are thought not to apply; still others the early church qualified or simply inverted, as the means of making them useful. It is astonishing how few of Jesus' words, in their original form, are suitable as a base for prudential moral reasoning.

The church did not, of course, set out on a program of systematic evasion. Quite to the contrary. The bewilderment and frustration of the church, like that of the modern interpreter, are not without real and cogent grounds. Jesus was explicit at those points where an excessive idealism robs his words of prudential force. He chose not to be explicit where he might have been most lucid in teaching man to live wisely and judiciously. Insofar as

80 Jesus' teachings are to be honored as the ground rules for a Christian ethic, reinterpretation, manipulation, supplementation seem to be not only permitted but actually required.

The following question is almost inevitable: if Jesus solicited obedience, why was he not more helpful in his formulations? Then the further question: did Jesus deliberately teach in such a way as to inhibit literal and direct compliance?

These questions may be explored in connection with the examination of an apothegm (Bultmann), paradigm (Dibelius), or pronouncement story (Vincent Taylor). The pericope on tribute to Caesar (Mk 12:13-17//Mt 22:15-22//Lk 20:20-26) may be taken as the choice example. Form critics generally agree that this pericope represents the apothegm in a nearly pure state.

Two preliminary remarks may be permitted.

The apothegm, in its pure form, stands very near the threshold of the tradition. Perhaps the first form to be utilized for transmitting the Jesus tradition, that does not go back to Jesus himself, is the apothegm. This form provides a minimal narrative context for a dominical saying, to put it concisely. Every other interest is subordinated to this function.

The question has never been raised to what extent the oral forms, utilized or invented by the primitive community as vehicles for the Jesus tradition, comport in both form and content with that tradition. For example, does the apothegm comport in essential respects with the parable? Although the matter cannot be pursued directly, the analysis of the apothegm on tribute will have this question constantly in view. It comes to attention by reason of the dilemma, referred to previously, to which the parable contributes so much, viz. the bewilderment and frustration over Jesus' lack of explicitness.

The pericope on tribute to Caesar, by virtue of its ostensible subject matter, represents a prime example of that frustration. Günther Bornkamm has drawn attention to a singular fact: this scene is the only place in the Gospels where the problem of the power of the state is mentioned. Indeed, the great Roman Empire figures only marginally in the gospel narrative (120). How do we

account for the strange silence of Jesus on what must have been a
burning issue for many Jews of his day? Jesus' lack of sensitivity to
the pervasive question of the relation of political and religious life
must have been as baffling then as it is now.

One common but misleading response to this question should
be dealt with here. It will not do to respond: Jesus ducked such
problems because of his anticipation of the approaching reign of
God. Bornkamm himself rightly observes: for Jesus, "this actual
world does not lose its contours in the glare of the last day" (121).

The famous epigram on tribute, "Render to Caesar the things
that are Caesar's, and to God the things that are God's," for the
sake of which the story was formed, is simply frustrating. To be
sure, the tradition of interpretation has tended to understand the
saying as an affirmation of the proprietary rights of Caesar. That
Jesus appended a pious word about obligations to God is to be
expected of a religious teacher and weighted accordingly. Yet so
simple a reading satisfies only those who have already made up
their minds to pay the tax. For the rest, the double
pronouncement is utterly perplexing. ·

The epigram or pronouncement of Jesus is set in a minimal
narrative context. In this case, the intuition that the epigram is
dark or puzzling goes together with the setting. Looking
backward from the concluding saying, Jesus' request for a coin
strikes one as odd, the reader notes that the question put to him is
loaded, and the opening speech of the interlocutors is
demonstrably a farce. Is there solid ground anywhere in the
account, or is the interpreter left with the shifting sands of
ambiguity? Perhaps rereading will help.

The first sentence, which is editorial introduction (0.), may be
set aside.

82

The Question Concerning Tribute to Caesar
Mark 12: 13-17

0.   [13]And they sent to him some of the Pharisees and some of the Herodians, to entrap him in his talk.

1.1   [14]And they came and said to him, "Teacher, we know that you are true, and care for no man; for you do not regard the position of men, but truly teach the way of God.

1.2   Is it lawful to pay taxes to Caesar, or not? [15]Should we pay them, or should we not?"

2.1   But knowing their hypocrisy, he said to them, "Why put me to the test?

2.2   Bring me a coin and let me look at it." [16]And they brought one. And he said to them, "Whose likeness and inscription is this?" They said to him, "Caesar's."

3.   [17]Jesus said to them, "Render to Caesar the things that are Caesar's, and to God the things that are God's."

4.   And they were amazed at him.

The opening words of the opponents (1.1) may be characterized as ironic: "Rabbi, we know you are true, that you don't give a rap for anyone's favor, that rank does not impress you, and that you teach God's way without equivocation." If this setting is authentic, this speech means something like the opposite of what it says. It is irony in its simplest form.

The ironic statement, in its simplest form, is a transparent lie. A lie, of course, is meant to deceive. The ironic statement is not. In Mark Anthony's famous speech, Act III, Scene ii of Shakespeare's *Julius Caesar*, there is a well-known example of irony:

> But Brutus says he was ambitious;
> And Brutus is an honorable man.

Anthony was scarcely in a position to speak the literal truth, so he spoke it ironically. That is, he told a transparent lie. The trend of his speech makes clear what he is about. Nevertheless, he is still dependent upon his hearers to gather what he really means.

Jesus' questioners dissemble in order to set the trap: "If you are all these things," they begin, "as your friends standing here seem to think, then you can and will answer our question, in the terms on which we ask it." Meanwhile, they are thinking to themselves: "If you do so, however, we've got you. If you tell us to pay the tribute, you will lose favor with the people; if you tell us to refuse, you will be in trouble with the secular authorities. Either way you lose."

The terms of the game are clear: a web of transparent lies, told for the sake of a crowd sympathetic to Jesus, is advanced as bait for a carefully conceived dilemma. The audience may not understand the name of the game, but Jesus does. And his interlocutors do: they hope, by the answer Jesus gives, that the irony of their lavish praise will become transparent, even to his illiterate followers.

So much is universally accepted. However, exegetes tend, at this point, to skip to the pronouncement (3.), which they then struggle to read two ways at once: first, as an evasion of the trap, and secondly, as advice to pay the tax. In that case, one is prompted to ask whether something was wrong with the trap. No interpreter, so far as is known, so understands the text. And yet there is a curious ambivalence: Jesus tells his hearers to pay the tax, but does not answer the question asked. It is difficult to see how the interpreter can have it both ways at once.

It is doubtful that the pronouncement is as ambiguous as most commentators seem to think. Bornkamm again calls attention to the critical point: had Jesus intended to give an unequivocal and explicit answer to the question, he would have said, "Give to Caesar what belongs to Caesar " (122). Better yet, he could have said, "Yes." But he does not. He constructs instead a couplet and produces what Schweitzer and Dibelius call "ironical parallelism" (Schweitzer: 314). What this term means is not clear, but it may be taken to mean that the two lines in juxtaposition mean something which the two lines taken separately do not. However that may be,

84   on no count is Jesus' reply straightforward and unequivocal, in relation to the question asked.

The pronouncement of Jesus, in some sense, subverts the question to which it is ostensibly the answer. And it is from this fundamental point of reference that one must go back and look at the intervening scene (2.).

In the controversy dialogues between Jesus and his opponents, the leading question is regularly followed by a counter-question or its surrogate. One of these surrogates is the demonstration or symbolic act (Bultmann: 44). In this apothegm, which takes the form of a controversy dialogue, the attack is followed by the scene in which Jesus asks for a coin. This scene is rarely understood.

Recall that Jesus' questioners have set a trap for him by means of ironic praise and a loaded question. He is aware of what they are up to, as his initial reply to the question indicates (2.1): "Why do you hold my feet to the iron?" That is a free translation meaning: "This is verbal torture designed to lead to self-incrimination." The next thing he does is ask for a coin.

Given this setting and one's knowledge of the form of the controversy dialogue, the reader may anticipate that Jesus' response will follow the track of the question, but in such a way as to go though an open switch. In railroad parlance that means: his response will follow the question, but end by breaking it open, by working against the question itself.

The scene (2.2) can best be represented by paraphrase.

"Does someone in the audience have a quarter," J. asks, like the amateur magician about to perform a disappearing trick. "I don't seem to have one on me."

Someone passes a two-bit piece forward.

J. holds the coin up for all to see. "Whose picture is that?" he inquires, and "What does the writing say?"

Nobody is fooled by this piece of showmanship. J. knows very well that the head is Washington's and that the inscription is the national motto. Nevertheless, he waits for an answer.

The fellow who had furnished the coin, thinking himself a precocious student, blurts out, "Washington's."

"Well, well. Imagine that," J. concludes, and pockets the quarter.

If subsequent readers had witnessed this scene just as Jesus' audience — apart from the dense and literalminded — witnessed it, there is not the slightest doubt that they would have understood it as ironic. It mirrors, and thus hands back, the irony of the preamble. The words and act mean something they do not literally say.

The little scene is ironic in order to suggest that the real question has to do, not with the rights of Caesar, but with the jurisdiction of God. But the legal mind, and the literal mind, demands its respects, which the wise man pays in ironic, metaphoric, or parabolic coin! The denarius makes its own claims, which are not ironic or metaphoric. For those enthralled by the question as posed, the answer of the denarius is answer enough.

To be sure, the ironic scene prepares the way for the pronouncement to come. Indeed, the first half of the epigram is designed as a special trap for those who missed the point of the demonstration. For those who see, however, that the question has been subverted, the epigram carries other implications.

On its surface, the epigram is disarmingly simple: pay Caesar what is his, and God what is his. Nothing could be plainer. All you have to do, Jesus advises, is determine what belongs to Caesar and what belongs to God. And there is where the difficulty with the question lies. Bornkamm puts it this way:

> But the very fact that here the entire problem of the state is thus put in the margin, and that its fundamental problems are not allowed to come to the surface, is obviously a very important word on the whole matter.
>
> (123)

And that very important word is that the questions of Caesar and God are really incommensurate. The kingdom about which Jesus speaks is the reign of God. On that *horizon*, the claims of Caesar are marginal, scarcely worth noticing at all. His hearers will understand that if they understand anything he has been saying at all. Consequently, the pronouncement shifts the outcome to the

86 auditor, by means of the inocuous "and": each must decide whether he is properly disposed to the root issue, the reign of God.

III

The analysis of the pericope on tribute indicates that the irony of Jesus and the reign of God were internally related. Irony was characterized as non-explicit language, and the reign of God was referred to as a horizon. The relation of non-explicit language to horizon requires exploration, in order to suggest how the need of new ancestors, land, mystery is joined to the need of a new language, in the case of John Fowles, and how the coming of the reign of God is related to irony, metaphor, parable, and other non-explicit modes of discourse, in the case of Jesus.

The link has already been suggested by the apothegm on tribute. The tax question as posed cannot be answered by Jesus because it has been wrongly framed. It has been asked in the wrong horizon. His response, accordingly, is directed, not to the question, but to the horizon. One may infer that to speak about horizon is to speak non-explicitly.

What is a horizon? Literally, a horizon is the limit or boundary of sight (from *horizein*, to fix boundaries, limits). The visible horizon is the apparent junction of earth and sky that circumscribes the field of vision. As boundary, horizon is non-explicit: it is not something in the field of vision, about which something definite can be said; it is rather the limits of the explicit.

Horizon has also come to mean the range of perception and experience. In this so-called figurative sense, horizon refers to the field of vision and experience itself, to what has been seen and experienced, and therefore to what can be seen and experienced. If it is said, "Witchcraft falls outside the horizon of the scientific mind," it is implied that only phenomena of a certain order can fall within that horizon. What falls outside cannot be seen and experienced, unless the phenomenon in question has an analogy within the range already established. The figurative sense thus also involves a boundary, albeit a boundary defined by the internal order of the sensibility — the range of its habituated expectations.

Horizons are subject to modification, to be sure. When a new perception is admitted, when the boundary is overstepped, the field of vision as a whole undergoes modification. A modification in horizon entails a modification in the order of the sensible field. Such modifications may be imperceptible, taking place obliquely over a period of time, as the horizon evolves. Or they may be radical, as when a single perception or experience shakes the order of the field to its foundations. The slower, evolutionary modification is the more common, since individual horizons are dominated by the collective consciousness, that is, they are socially conditioned and sustained.

At one point in the *Tractatus Logico-Philosophicus* (5.61), Ludwig Wittgenstein claims that language and world are co-extensive. The limits of language means the limits of world: this, he says, cannot be demonstrated, but shows itself. In another place (4.12ff.), he writes:

> That which mirrors itself in language, language itself cannot represent. That which expresses *itself* in language, *we* cannot express by language.

This doctrine of Wittgenstein is very difficult, and he may have abandoned it later in his career. Nevertheless, he appears to connect the limits of language, i.e. of what can be said explicitly, with the limits of world, or with the horizon. In other words, explicit language is restricted to what falls within the horizon.

Wittgenstein offers this laconic explanation: "Logic fills the world: the limits of the world are also its limits. We cannot therefore say in logic, this and this there is in the world, *that* there is not . . . since otherwise logic must get outside the limits of the world . . . " (5.61). Now, if logic cannot get outside the world, it obviously cannot specify the limits of world. On the contrary, the limits of world mark the limits of logic. Nevertheless, the limits of language and world *show* themselves. How is that possible?

Wittgenstein suggests that his own efforts in the *Tractatus* are aimed at saying what cannot be said:

88

> My propositions serve as elucidations in the following way:
> anyone who understands me eventually recognizes them as
> nonsensical, when he has used them — as steps — to climb
> beyond them. (He must, so to speak, throw away the ladder
> after he has climbed up it.)
>
> He must understand these propositions, and then he will see
> the world aright.
>
> What we cannot speak about we must consign to silence.
>
> (6.54, 7)

Wittgenstein appears to be saying here that his own explicit
language in the *Tractatus* is ultimately to be viewed as
nonsensical, since, in following out the logic of explicit language,
he has endeavored to climb out beyond explicit language. That
move takes him into the realm of non-explicit language — termed
nonsensical from the perspective of explicit language — and thus
beyond the limits of the world, the horizon. Although the
Tractatus presumably contains only explicit language, as a whole
it is *inexplicit*: it points beyond itself, to what cannot be said, to
what must be consigned to silence.

Wittgenstein has in mind, of course, the world of atomic facts
and the fully explicit language analytic philosophers were
constructing to go with that world. There are at hand, however,
other, less abstract means of elucidating the same basic notions.

One might, for example, consider the Victorian world inherited
by Nicolas Urfe. In place of Wittgenstein's logical language, one
could describe certain characteristic features of that world, or one
could put those features in narrative form, as John Fowles has
done in another of his novels, *The French Lieutenant's Woman*. If
the Victorian legacy is still alive in the reader, or if he is sufficiently
literate, he will be able to grasp, imaginatively, the Victorian
world precisely as horizon. However, please observe, he will not
have grasped that world, as horizon, because that horizon has
been put explicitly into words. Rather, by virtue of certain explicit
points on a spectrum, the range and order of the spectrux as a
whole will have suggested itself. The horizon has not been
demonstrated, but shows itself.

Similarly, attention may be directed to certain features of

everyday life in late antiquity, say, in Palestine in the time of Jesus. But no number of such particulars will delineate the shape of that world, that horizon: the horizon of life and language in that period cannot be said, but shows itself, that is, explodes, at some point, in the imagination, into a kind of ordered limit. And the curious thing about it is this: when that horizon has come to life for one person, through intensive study and imaginative completion, that person will be unable to convey that horizon to someone else, except by the same process.

Prose fiction offers a further illustration. The author of a novel never tells the whole story. How could he? To do so would require an infinity of words. What he does is to provide the cardinal points on the narrative compass, and the reader fills in freely out of his own imagination. The skill of the novelist lies in his ability to awaken the imagination to the horizon of the story. The reader writes the rest of it himself, within that horizon. In fact, the novelist himself is subject to the same limitations: he establishes the characters and the situation — the horizon; the creatures of his imagination then take over, in their own freedom, and play out the drama for him.

One may therefore say: the story is not told, the hellenistic world, the Victorian horizon, are not said, but each is permitted to show itself. The horizon of any world cannot be put into words. Were it possible to say a world in an infinity of words, a world so specified in language would not be living, but dead; not a place of human activity, but a wax museum.

Jesus, it is said, came proclaiming the reign of God. The reign to which his words pointed was not accompanied by observable signs. Men could not say, "There it is!" or "Here it is!" (Lk 17:20). Those about him, though craning their necks, could not see what he was talking about. Because they could not see it, they were inclined to think the reign to which he pointed was unreal. They did not know and could not guess that they were under the spell of another horizon. However, the poor and the destitute, the tax collectors and prostitutes saw it, and rejoiced. For them, Jesus' magic was stronger than the magic of habituated sensibility.

90   The invisibility of the reign of God has nothing to do with the contrast between outward and inner, between physical and spiritual. It has rather to do with that world or limit or horizon, to which Wittgenstein alludes: in proclaiming the reign of God, Jesus is pronouncing a new horizon for human existence. As horizon, it cannot be put into words, but may show itself.

It should now be clear why ironic, metaphoric, and parabolic language came so readily to Jesus' lips. These modes of language point beyond themselves, to what cannot be said; they refuse to come to rest in the literal, the particular, the propositional, the casuistic. To criticisms, questions, situations, friendly and hostile, Jesus steadily refused to respond within the horizon of the received world. Instead, he referred his critics and friends, by means of non-explicit language, to the world, the horizon, which was real and ultimate for him — the reign of God.

Modern frustration with and bewilderment at Jesus is thus not without good reason: one expects him to say something, and he refuses. Yet by speaking in parables, riddles, and enigmas, he made it as hard as possible to be misunderstood. He is misread because interpreters trample over his words with their own demands for explicitness. But he never fills in what cannot be filled in without damning his followers to a living death. Understanding of the horizon, of the reign of God, lies beyond the frontier of what can be said: who would venture into those precincts must go without benefit of explicit verbal instructions.

IV

Nicolas Urfe failed to reach that enchanted shore, from which could be seen islands and princesses. In the end he fell back on the legacy he wished to disown. Similarly, the mass of those in whom the Victorian legacy and Consciousness II — to use the term of Charles Reich — lives on, the Parents and Teachers of today, continue, for the most part, to act out a period morality play, with antique props and quaint dialogue, now overlaid with the dirty grime of the industrial state. The PTA should be able to offer the new generation one assurance: there is no truth beyond magic. It learned or should have learned that there are many kinds of magic, and that there is no way to arbitrate, penultimately, between and among them. This knowledge should be the product of the grand disillusionment, stemming from two world wars and the economic bust of the 30's. Yet the PTA has not passed this fundamental insight on, but has thoughtlessly perpetuated a previous illusion as THE TRUTH. As a consequence, today's children are in revolt against a hoax.

It is a point that the very young should bear in mind when seeking their way in the world. To locate one's self in the world, to draw near a new land and time, one must first of all determine who one's parents are. That is not an easy assignment, especially for orphans. Orphans should beware: unidentified or unacknowledged parents are, willy-nilly, the most tyrannous kind.

On this point Jesus cannot be faulted. He knew perfectly well who his parents were: not Joseph and Mary, but the scribes and Pharisees. That is the reason we hear so much of them in the Gospels.

The lesson the generation of Nicolas Urfe struggled to learn is that it is not enough to revolt against the past, to disown one's hands. Disowning is saying perpetual goodbye to one's ancestors; it is bidding farewell to that by virtue of which one belongs to a time and place, to a land and race and language. But disowning is also saying hello to one's forbearers. It is the poet's hail of a new time and place, by virtue of a reconstituted past. Histories are never discarded. They either tyrannize as a fate, or they are transformed, from time to time, into the threshold of a new future.

While Jesus was bidding goodbye to the Pharisees, he was saying hello to Moses and the prophets; he was reconstituting the legacy of Israel. In a form, to be sure, that those who thought they knew that legacy best scarcely recognized.

Jesus was certainly a word magician. He intended to create a world as real as, but other than, the world that was, as John Fowles suggests with reference to the craft of the novelist (*French*

92   *Lieutenant's Woman*: 96). He was one of the poets Shelley had in mind when he quoted Tasso with approval: "None but God and the Poet deserves the name of Creator" (Schorer: 469). Nevertheless, Jesus did not impose the reign of God upon his hearers. He merely let it show itself. The responsibility for seeing and hearing rested entirely with them: who has ears to hear, let him hear. And each man was free to enter in upon that reign in accordance with his ownmost destiny. Most important of all, the mystery of the kingdom was to remain perpetually intact: the horizon of the reign of God did not parade itself as THE TRUTH, but remained transparent to its own beyond, to the mystery of the horizon of horizons.

Jesus as Saunterer

Sauntering and the Sacred:
Coming to our Senses (Henry David Thoreau)

Jesus as Saunterer

Sauntering and the Sacred:
Coming to One's Senses

I

What sort of walk is it from Concord to Jerusalem, from New England to the Holy Land? Henry David Thoreau thought it not far, to the west, as he reckoned, since the Holy Land was the object of his daily walks, and the sacred place lay in the wilderness west of Concord, as he supposed everyone knew.

Thoreau was a surveyor, among other things. His use of level and line was discriminating: he knew there were many things in heaven and earth the measure of which no surveyor could take. To take the true lie of the land a poet was required. And for sense of direction one had to rely on dead reckoning. Poetry and reckoning were arts to be cultivated on walks — walks, that is, to the Holy Land.

In his essay on "Walking," published in 1862, Thoreau ventures to speak a word for "Nature," by which he means a word "for absolute freedom and wildness" (597). In so doing, Thoreau proposes to consider man as part and parcel of Nature, rather than as a member of society. Of champions of civilization there are enough, he says; what is needed is a champion of the free and

96   wild. So he enters himself in the lists on behalf of the untamed, the unmanaged, the unimpoverished.

Who is ready for a walk, asks Thoreau? He answers,

> If you are ready to leave father and mother, and brother and sister, and wife and child and friends, and never see them again, — if you have paid your debts, and made your will, and settled all your affairs, and are a free man, then you are ready for a walk.

(598)

In short, only the authentically free man is ready for a walk, and, conversely, only the saunterer is a free man. One must understand, of course, that the walking of which Thoreau speaks "has nothing in it akin to taking exercise" ("Walking": 600).

The saunterer is a special species of walker. The saunterer is a pilgrim on his way to the Holy Land, so to speak. The term *sauntering* is derived, Thoreau instructs us, from the idlers who roamed about Europe during the Middle Ages begging alms on the pretext of going *à la Sainte Terre*, to the Holy Land. The sight became so familiar children were wont to exclaim, "There goes a *Sainte-Terrer*," a Saunterer, a Holy Lander. Now, of course, those who only pretended to go to the Holy Land were really vagabonds, vagrants, not saunterers. The true saunterer is indeed on a holy crusade (597f.).

If the saunterer is in quest of the sacred place, on his way to the Holy Land, in which direction shall he set out, and for what sort of country shall he look?

"When I go out of the house for a walk," writes Thoreau, ". . . I finally and inevitably settle southwest. . . . The future lies that way to me, and the earth seems more unexhausted and richer on that side" (607). He insists he must walk toward Oregon and not toward Europe; that he cannot bear to recross the Atlantic, to retrace the steps of his ancestors to a soil now worn out and used up (608). He is irresistibly drawn to "the Great *West* of the Ancients, enveloped in mystery and poetry" (609). When gazing into the sunset of a western sky, who has not seen the gardens of the Hesperides, the Eden of paganism that lay on the horizons of the west?

For Thoreau the reason to flee the Old World and its tradition was not so much that it had been over-rationalized, as was the case with the lesser romantics. It was rather that the bloom of European arts and letters had begun to fade for lack of earthy nourishment. It was not always so. "Mythology is the crop which the Old World bore before its soil was exhausted," he claims, "before the fancy and imagination were affected with blight" (620). The condition of the soil and the health of the imagination are here connected, both in literal and figurative senses. A raped and ravished earth lacks the power to fire the imagination, and an imagination that is not rooted in the earth, that is not autochthonous, is diseased, soon to perish. Without the marriage of the earth and man's fancy, mythologies wither and die.

Thoreau's move was thus away from civilization, from the *villa*, which, he says, is related to the *vile* and the *villain*, from the habituated, faded and jaded sensibility of the Old World. His move was simultaneously toward the wild, toward the wilderness, toward that reality which steals the initiative from the imagination and charges it afresh with power.

On these terms it is possible to understand why the mythical West of which Thoreau speaks is another name for the Wild. The West is away from crystallized culture and ossified tradition; the wilderness is unfettered and undomesticated reality. He who would go west must therefore seek the wild in order to front the real. When the imagination perceives the real, it will be found to be "fabulous." So fabulous a reality simply overpowered Thoreau; he stood in awe beside Walden Pond, like Adam in the Garden. It is for these reasons, Thoreau insists, "that in Wildness is the preservation of the World" (613).

So far from being inimical to civilization, the wild is actually ingredient to the health of society. It is no meaningless fable, Thoreau says, that Romulus and Remus were suckled by a wolf, and it is understandable that the children of the northern forests later overran the children of the Empire, who spent too much time indoors (613). And, Thoreau would add, it is not by chance that

98 Israel was born in the wilderness, nor is it surprising that the prophets again and again called the people of God back to the ways of the desert.

Given the choice between a garden and a swamp, Thoreau unhesitatingly chose the swamp. He entered the swamp as a *sanctum sanctorum*, for here was "the strength, the marrow of Nature" (616). Proximity to a swamp or forest is no less necessary for man than it is for the wild animals (617). A town is redeemed, not by its righteous men, but by "the woods and swamps that surround it" (617). The ideal setting is a town with a primitive forest waving above and another rotting underfoot; "such a town," Thoreau writes, "is fitted to raise not only corn and potatoes, but poets and philosophers for the coming ages. In such a soil grew Homer and Confucius and the rest, and out of such a wilderness comes the Reformer eating locusts and wild honey" (617).

Thoreau perceived the internal relation between and among sauntering, the sacred and the senses, and so makes his confession:

> I perceive that we inhabitants of New England live this mean life that we do because our vision does not penetrate the surface of things. We think that that *is* which *appears* to be."
>
> (*Walden*: 87)

The daily life of routine and habit is based on illusion and shadows because it is divorced from the real. But

> reality is fabulous. If men would steadily observe realities only, and not allow themselves to be deluded, life, to compare it with such things as we know, would be like a fairy tale and the Arabian Nights' Entertainments. If we respected only what has a right to be, music and poetry would resound along the streets."
>
> (*Walden*: 86)

The art of discerning the "realities only" may best be cultivated by walking or sauntering. Thoreau says pointedly: "In my walks I would fain return to my senses" (602). On his walks he aspires to "wedge his feet downward through the mud and slush of opinion, and prejudice, and tradition, and delusion, and appearance, that alluvion which covers the globe, . . . till we come to a hard bottom and rocks in place, which we call *reality*, and say, This is, and no mistake" (*Walden*: 88). But that reality of which Thoreau speaks is not our scientific fact, our hard and polished datum; it is the bush aflame at the sacred mountain, it is the Kingdom of God, it is that fabulous yonder which provokes poetry and music and dancing. In sum, that reality is the sacred.

II

On Thoreau's terms, it may fairly be claimed that Jesus was a man ready for a walk, who was, indeed, already sauntering along toward Jerusalem, the Holy City.

Even by Thoreau's standards Jesus was a *free* man: he had said goodbye to mother and father, to wife and children, to brothers and sisters. He did not even bother with Thoreau's shack by Walden Pond; he had nowhere to lay his head. The morrow was bidden to look out for itself, and the dead were left to bury the dead.

Jesus was also free in the sense that he was headed *west*: away from the depleted tradition, away from the scribes and Pharisees who reinforced the loss, away from stereotyped expectations. Jesus never invokes the fathers in support of his dicta (Bornkamm: 97), and he declares that the tradition of the Pharisees in fact makes void the word of God (Mk 7:13 par). More importantly, Jesus reverses prevailing anticipations: the tax collectors and the prostitutes go into the Kingdom but the righteous do not (Mt 21:31); those invited to the banquet make excuses, so the hall is filled with the destitute; the wayward son returns to the embrace of his father, while the proper son pouts without.

With Jesus, too, the west is another name for the *wild*. Jesus came out of the wilderness in the company of John, and was never far from it. Like Thoreau, Jesus often withdrew in solitude. Further, he no doubt would have agreed with Thoreau that "there is something in the mountain-air that feeds the spirit and inspires"

100 (611). In short, Jesus was braced to the chilling dawn of the desert and the sheer austerity of the craggy heights.

On several counts, then, the credentials of Jesus would satisfy Thoreau. But it would be a mistake to press the analogy, with Thoreau as the primary term. Where sight and the sacred are concerned, Jesus does not play a different tune, but he does compose in another key.

It was observed that for Thoreau the Holy Land lay in the wilderness to the west of Concord. Jesus, on the other hand, appears to locate the sacred in the interstices of the everyday, the commonplace, the mundane.

The parables present us, for the most part, with a carefully selected cross-section of hum-drum existence — carefully selected because these pictures catch man and things in their most typical postures, yet at just those junctures where a significant 'turn' is possible. The householder is routinely engaged in hiring and harvesting: who could have anticipated that his activities, which are gradually and subtly exaggerated, would explode into a fundamental choice about the hearer's relation to his destiny? It does not dawn on us until much later that the lowly and familiar mustard plant constitutes a burlesque of Ezekiel's mighty cedar of Israel. The prospect of a forgotten treasure in an orchard or field is not entirely remote, as any budding Palestinian archaeologist will assure you. Imagine the flood of joy that gathers around the rare fulfillment of that prospect and one has some premonition of what Thoreau and Jesus thought they had discovered on a solitary stroll abroad.

These pictures and others like them — the salt, the lamp on the stand, the barren fig tree — open before the eyes as apertures onto the ultimate. Yet they do not lose their mundaneness. As Amos Wilder notes, one looks in vain among the parables and aphorisms of Jesus for the romantic, the sentimental, for false mysticism and escape into fantasy; there is only the real, the actual, the natural. Jesus' narratives and figures "stay close to things as they are" (74). It is this peculiar conflation of the ordinary and sacred — virtually impossible to duplicate — that characterizes the words — and public life — of Jesus.

Ernest Käsemann suggests that Jesus abolished "the difference, basic for the ancient world, between the temenos, the sacred area, and the profane world." For this reason, he felt himself free to keep company with prostitutes and sinners (Bornkamm: 98). But it also means that the locus of the sacred had shifted for him, from the temple to the marketplace, from the synagogue to the crossroads.

The ability to discern the sacred in the secular, in the common, depends on an uncommon set of perceptions, and this in two respects. Jesus (and Thoreau) were apparently able to *divine* the holy in the common because the latter presented them with at least two faces. As Thoreau has it, when properly fronting a 'fact', one discerns "the sun glimmer on *both* its surfaces," and one then feels its "sweet edge dividing you through the heart and marrow" (*Walden*: 88). An uncommon confrontation with reality is conjoined with an equally uncommon awareness of background, of the frame of the picture, one might say, of the horizon. Needless to say, the one discrimination goes together with the other.

The *horizon* of Jesus' perception of the commonplace he called the Kingdom of God. The lilies of the field, the sower broadcasting seed, the unmerciful servant are *placed* with reference to the kingdom. How is that possible?

The chairman of the Art Department at the University of Montana was told, in the fourth memorandum, that he had to specify the location of the new mimeograph machine he had just purchased; it was a university requirement. To this demand he replied: "It is located in my outer office, just right of the south window, next to the flower pot." He had learned, perhaps from Thoreau, that a fence does not *bound* a field any more than occupation or parents or address *place* a man. Herman Melville tells us that the pagan harpooner, Queequeg, was from an island in the far away Pacific. "It is not down on any map; true places never are" (54). Which is to say, real places are marked, not by undifferentiated space, but by qualified space. The Kingdom of God qualifies the space in which Jesus dwells.

102   Jesus places things by that onto which they open. The road to Jericho opens onto the neighbor, onto the humanity of man, onto the ultimate. Most travellers see only a dusty, precipitous, and treacherous road, perhaps with a robber's victim in the ditch. Jesus saw someone beckoning across the chasm of man's indifference, preoccupation, and bigotry. The facts of the case have at least two faces.

It should not be supposed that the metaphor by which things find their true place is like a pair of glasses one slips on for the occasion. The kingdom for Jesus and the wild for Thoreau are not aids to sight; *they are sight*. The kingdom is not the frame around a picture which all men see; it is the picture itself. What Jesus and Thoreau see is really different. Reality is fabulous, as Thoreau puts it. This is the significance of the fact that when Jesus calls attention to the ordinary — the seed growing, the friend pounding on the door at midnight, two men at prayer — he does not intend that we should think of something else, such as religion, or synagogue, or God. He intends that we should see what he sees, there, in the things himself. The wall of the temenos is broken down; the sacred has come to dwell in the common and ordinary.

III

From this point on the way west is less well marked. One dares to venture further because there is ample wilderness to be explored. For guidance one is forced to rely on a few additional signposts, some with very faded legends. First, the laconic markers; subsequently, halting and fragmentary notations.

1. Jesus and Thoreau appear to have this in common: both aspired to a direct *confrontation with the bedrock of reality*. In passing: is it possible that the quest for the real is a "religious" quest?

2. The reality Jesus and Thoreau seek is not, however, our brute, scientific fact, the unadorned *Ding-an-sich*, but the *horizon* in which things find their places and hence faces.

3. Reality as horizon is to be discovered by the releasement of

things: things populating the field of vision are released from the tyranny of sight, so that blind eyes may catch sight of the horizon of things. Thoreau's "fronting of facts" was really "the nearness of distance" (Heidegger). One must get back far enough to able to see up close; one must not look too hard lest one miss the sight.

4. Man's quest of the horizon is dependent upon the thrust and guidance system of his *language*; the thrust and guidance system of language depends, in turn, upon the purity of the act of releasement.

These propositions abut, perhaps trample on or knock down, the natural piety of Thoreau and the religion of Jesus. To promise to elucidate them in language other than the cramped jargon in which they are stated is a challenge unlikely to be met.

The Jesus of the Fourth Gospel is the light-bringer: he causes the blind to see. The sight he brings is new light on six stone jars at the wedding and the water in Jacob's well. At the conclusion of the episode of the man born blind (John 9), John has Jesus say, "For judgment I came into this world, that those who do not see may see, and that those who see may become blind" (Jn 9:39). The root meaning of *judgment* (*krima*) is *discernment*: Jesus precipitates real sight, thereby exposing habituated sight for what it really is, viz. blindness.

Of the blindness of the world Thoreau was also deeply aware:

> By closing the eyes and slumbering, and consenting to be deceived by shows, men establish and confirm their daily life of routine and habit everywhere, which still is built on purely illusory foundations.
>
> (*Walden*: 86)

Where Jesus speaks of blindness, Thoreau speaks of slumbering. Thoreau complains: "I have never yet met a man who was quite awake" (*Walden*: 81). He yearns for a perpetual inward morning, in which facts scintillate in kalaedescopic beauty under a fresh sun.

The natural piety of Thoreau may be summed up thus: "I got up early and bathed in the pond; that was a religious exercise, and one of the best things which I did" (*Walden*: 80). The religion of

Jesus had to do, too, with earthly things; the earthly things of which Jesus spoke were so fabulous he never quite got around to heavenly things (Jn 3:12).

Such hunger for the real is fed, in the sensitive soul, by the bread and water of certain sight. The unambiguous fact may be set down as a sham and a delusion; it is made unequivocal and univocal by virtue of restricted horizons. The many faces of things owe to the changing, undulating light of countless suns rising over limitless horizons.

Thoreau boasted that he had traveled much in Concord. Which is to say, Concord put on a new face for every stroll, and the supply of masks seemed inexhaustible. Jesus apparently was also an eager traveler: ever enroute to a fresh confrontation, but never with a final destination. The reality Jesus and Thoreau seek is the horizon by which things find their true places and hence real faces.

It was said that reality as horizon is discovered with the releasement of things. The circumspections that attend the horizon are precipitated by a releasement of things previously held in the foreground of consciousness. It is as though one may not focus simultaneously on the near at hand and the horizon; to attend the one is to lose sight of the other.

The preceding generalization needs to be qualified in at least this respect: the field of awareness is never empty; attention to horizon means that the focus on objects in the foreground is *soft* (Philip Wheelwright) rather than sharp.

The parables of Jesus are circumspections of the horizon or horizons of things. This is the reason the details of the narrative picture, though set out with intense realism, cannot be pressed: they invite attention, not to themselves, but to the horizon, just as the painting leads our eye unfalteringly to the vanishing point. Of the painting, for instance, the animals painted on the walls of Lascaux, Merleau-Ponty writes: "It is more accurate to say that I see according to it, or with it, than that I *see it*" (164). The parable and the painting draw the eye, by means of a skillfully arranged soft focus on objects in the foreground, to the horizon by virtue of which those objects gain their places and faces. Thus, the objects

in the foreground previously released again become the object of
attention, but within a new horizon and undergirded and
protected by fresh integrity. The relation between object and
horizon is a spiral, to use the figure of Ray Hart.

Releasement of and toward things is actually one integral act.
Given this time and place, however, one should probably
concentrate on releasement *of.* Given the subject matter (religion),
one may observe that the question is often conceived
theologically.

From the Fourth Gospel and Paul we learn that the "Jews" (in a
metaphorical sense: substitute Presbyterian, Methodist, Puritan,
or whatever) are those who pervert "creation" into man's "world"
by the instrument of religion. The Jews take possession of what
was given them as the basis of a claim against the giver. Our
righteousness, as Paul puts it, entitles man, so he thinks, to
something beyond what is already given him. Such arrogance
means that he does not wish to be put down as a creature, as part
and parcel of creation (of Nature, as Thoreau would say). By
setting oneself above creation, one ends by profaning the created
world — and oneself along with it. The earth and its creatures
become the instrument of man's self-exaltation. Creation is thus
perverted into the "world" of shadows, of self-deception, of
hubris.

The "Jews" have their secular counterpart in the modern West.
Since religion has been secularized, or, to put it more tellingly,
since the world has been dedivinized, shorn of the gods and spirits,
the whole creation has been taken in tow by man. The earth is
considered to be at the disposal of man. This man, for whom the
horizon is no longer open but restricted, stopped down, is driven
to make nature the instrument of his own self-administered
redemption and divinization.

This longing to subdue the land, to mark it off, strip it bare,
undermine it, leave it gasping for breath, the American Indian has
never quite understood. From the first contact of white and
redman in "New England," the notion of ownership puzzled the
Indian. Chief Joseph of the Nez Percés puts it pointedly:

106

> . . . The country was made without lines of demarcation, and it is no man's business to divide it. . . . Do not misunderstand me, but understand me fully with reference to my affection for the land. I never said the land was mine to do with as I chose. The one who has the right to dispose of it is the one who created it. I claim a right to live on my land, and accord you the privilege to live on yours.

The year was 1877, only 15 years after Thoreau's essay "On Walking." And Thoreau could not have put it better.

The conversation of Jesus with the rich young ruler (Lk 18:18ff.) is usually taken to turn on the question of the responsible stewardship of possessions. Yet Jesus demands that the young man, in addition to observing the commandments, sell all that he has and distribute it to the poor. The moral dilemma in which that places the church, when read literally, is excruciating! Let the moral dilemma stand for those for whom it is painful. For all others, Jesus is inviting to the releasement of things: to have as not having; not to have as having/to enjoy without possessing.

The venture which is here being spoken of is gotten underway and sustained by means of language. So crucial are the first words that one hesitates to pronounce them; the framing of even the question may make the quest abortive. Beyond the dangers of new and fragile life, there is always the threat that one's use of language will throttle the issue at the precise moment one is trying to breathe life into it.

By way of suggestion here are two incisive remarks of Thoreau.

> He would be a poet who could impress the winds and streams into his service, to speak for him; who nailed words to their primitive senses, as farmers drive down stakes in the spring, which the frost has heaved; who derived his words as often as he used them, — transplanted them to his page with earth adhering to their roots . . ..
>
> ("Walking": 619)

The relation to language which Thoreau commends seeks to restore man's rootedness, his autochthony, which Heidegger claims is under threat by the very spirit of the age. Words with earth adhering to their roots can be spoken only by men who are of the earth earthy. This relation to language is thus concomitant with the releasement toward things.

The second observation of Thoreau is this:

> It is too late to be studying Hebrew; it is more important to understand even the slang of today.
>
> ("Walking": 612)

Thoreau here states what biblical scholars have yet to discover: the language of the bible is a dead language. Rather than rehearse empty words in a mortified tongue, Thoreau suggests that it is more important to learn the current slang, that is, the living language. But the allusion should not be permitted to rest with the literal: Thoreau is also suggesting that the language we all speak daily, proximally and for the most part, is a dead language. Minimally, literacy means speaking and writing at least one living tongue.

It has been the aim of this essay to suggest that sauntering, the sacred, and the vitality of the senses are integrally related in Thoreau as in Jesus. To the extent that one may wish to speak of the concrete, e.g. the environmental crisis, one may speak of it only aspiringly, in the context of a maimed and depraved relation of man to the world about him. For the senses have become dull in the slumber of self-assertion. In the "air-conditioned nightmare" of the American, he has levelled reality with the bulldozer of exploitation and paved it over with inattention. It is time to take a walk and come to one's senses.

PART TWO

VOICES OF SILENCE

Voices of Silence

What are the shapes of silence?

    Silence is the embarrassment of nothing to say,
    Of muteness in a hungry void.

    Silence is the dots at the end of a broken sentence,
    Lineal witness to a vertical lack.

    Silence is the white that surrounds the black,
    The greater part of the page.

    Silence is the great refusal,
    The boisterous denial of compromise.

Silence is the consonant
Without a vowel mate.

Silence is language
In the throes of death.

Silence is inhaling
In the interstices of action. (Zen)

Silence is speech
Waiting to be born.

    Silence is what follows the splash
    Of the frog in the pond.

    Silence is the draped shape of snow
    After the storm.

    Silence is rustling leaves
    At dusk.

    Silence is what precedes
    The rise of a trout.

Silence is the literal
Damning the hearer by conundrum.

Silence is the metaphor
Anointing the future.

The literal is the silent
Temptation to rancid repetition.

The metaphor is the silent
Invitation to masturbation.

In a world of non-relations,
Silence is the non-syntax of monologue.

In a world of non-communication,
Silence is an approximation of the real.

Siren's Song Without Sound:
Linguistic Inversions on the Shores of Silence

Siren's Song Without Sound:
Linguistic Inversions on the Shores of Silence

The seductive goddess Circe advised Odysseus that he alone should hear the wonderful voices of the Sirens. His men were to bind him with strong ropes upright to the mast of the ship. Their own ears were to be stopped with wax. When the ineluctable song drifted across a becalmed sea to the tiny ship, Odysseus strained against his bonds; he commanded his crew to release him. His men, unhearing, tightened his ropes and rowed on.

So Homer recounts the saga, in Book Twelve.

The story of Odysseus and the Sirens did not reach the ears of Franz Kafka in precisely its Homeric form. As with many other marvelous tales of old, Kafka heard a slightly different version, which struck him, in this case, as a parable of his own supreme temptation.

Of Kafka's hearing, Odysseus thwarts the irresistible charm of the Siren's song with a stratagem at once both childish and supremely clever. Although the Siren's song could pierce anything, Odysseus naïvely stops his own ears with wax, has himself bound to the mast, and then sails within earshot in

117

innocent elation.

It is important, on Kafka's view, to understand the real threat posed by the Sirens to the homeward bound hero. He writes:

> Now the Sirens have a still more fatal weapon than their song, namely their silence. And though admittedly such a thing has never happened, still it is conceivable that someone might possibly have escaped from their singing; but from their silence certainly never.
>
> (*Parables and Paradoxes*: 89)

Moreover, Kafka continues,

> When Odysseus approached them the potent songstresses actually did not sing, whether because they thought that this enemy could be vanquished only by their silence, or because the look of bliss on the face of Odysseus, who was thinking of nothing but his wax and his chains, made them forget their singing.
>
> (89f.)

Against the prowess of Odysseus was pitted not merely the legendary potency of the Siren's song, but the uncanny power of their song without sound.

In the face of so overwhelming a threat, Odysseus had to bring into play all the ingenuity for which Homer made him famous. At Kafka's hand, this ingenuity is so superbly subtle that it is subject to interpretation: even the gods did not certainly know how Odysseus escaped. One version, according to Kafka, is this:

> But Odysseus, if one may so express it, did not hear their silence; he thought they were singing and that he alone did not hear them. For a fleeting moment he saw their throats rising and falling, their breasts lifting, their eyes filled with tears, their lips half-parted, but believed that these were accompaniments to the airs which died unheard around him.
>
> (91)

Deaf Odysseus, bound up and stopped down to elude the seductive song, in his innocence, slips through the fingers of that fatal silence.

But was Odysseus innocent of the real threat? To the foregoing interpretation, says Kafka, a codicil has also been handed down:

Odysseus, it is said, was so full of guile, was such a fox, that not even the goddess of fate could pierce his armor. Perhaps he had really noticed, although here the human understanding is beyond its depths, that the Sirens were silent, and opposed the afore-mentioned pretense to them and the gods merely as a sort of shield.

(91)

On this account, Odysseus knew the quarter where the real danger lurked, but chose to fend off that danger by a feigned defense against an ostensible threat. Being the fox that he was, his deception was double.

On the first version, Odysseus thought he did not hear the song he thought the Sirens were singing, and so was innocent of their silence. According to the second interpretation, he pretended he did not hear the song he pretended they were singing, and so was shielded, by his pretension, from their silence, against which his wax and chains were no defense at all.

In either case, the parable of Odysseus and the Sirens, for Kafka, was a parable of the ultimate poetic temptation, the temptation to fall dumb.

Kafka, too, stopped his ears and had himself bound. He struggled in vain not to hear what he thought he was hearing. But he lacked the heroic resources of an Odysseus. In contrast to the Homeric epic, the gods had not decreed that Kafka would reach his ancestral home. The noise of the world penetrated his defenses. He was fatefully beckoned, wax and all, down the road to solicitous silence.

I

Kafka died in 1924, leaving a modest literary legacy behind. That legacy he committed to his friend, Max Brod, with the following instructions:

> My last request: Everything I leave behind me . . . in the way of diaries, manuscripts, letters . . . , sketches, and so on, to be burned unread.
> (*The Trial*: 328, postscript to the first edition, 1925, by Max Brod)

Nothing could be more explicit: the silence Kafka had broken was to be literally restored.

Brod invented various pretexts, of course, for avoiding these categorical instructions. It is well that he did. The twentieth century would have been bereft of its Dante, Shakespeare, or Goethe, in the judgment of W. H. Auden, had Brod executed the wishes of his friend (Quoted by Steiner: 118). Yet neither the act of conservation nor the pronouncement are to be taken to mean that a full, resonant voice has spoken unequivocally to the present age. On the contrary, Kafka broke the silence in order to call attention to it all the more. Without his works we would not be able to hear the silence he heard, at least not as well. Kafka wrote what he thought it possible to write: every polished phrase is a tribute to the mute muse that summoned him; every considered cadence witnesses to the deafening silence that engulfed him. In Kafka silence descends eloquently.

Kafka critics have rightly insisted that Kafka was ambivalent as regards the publication of his work. He was torn between the impossibility of not writing and the impossibility of writing. He also found it impossible to write differently, and impossible to write in German (Steiner: 122). Because it was impossible not to write, he wrote. Because it was impossible to write, he ordered his work destroyed. Because he could not write differently, he feared that he would only add to the linguistic pollution that filled the air. Because it was impossible to write in German, he scoured that tongue with a wire brush, leaving it as barren of cultural deposit and metaphoric sediment as he could. And then, having written clean and naked prose he took back everything he said. The request to Brod to burn was the final, inevitable act of his feverish desire to let his voice fall unheard.

Kafka left the bulk of his work unfinished. His two major novels, *The Trial* and *The Castle*, are open ended. The arrangement of the chapters is uncertain. And revisions, alternate versions, deletions, and fragments abound. Perhaps his aesthetic perfectionism was a crippling master, as critics maintain. Yet Kafka seemed unable, for other reasons, to put a period to anything he wrote. A text with full punctuation is possible only in an age that has made up its mind. Kafka had not. His stories and novels, even his revisitation of the ancient myths, run out into an infinity of further qualification. One is reminded of Samuel Beckett's bent for the assertion with a question mark at the end, or the question followed by a period. Not the period but a series of dots . . . . . is appropriate to a writer who has silence as his destiny.

Like many an author before him, Kafka speaks of "false hands" beckoning him away from his course (*The Trial*: 327, postscript by Max Brod). He insists that what he has written constitutes an impediment to further work. The need to destroy as he went attests not so much to the rigor of his aesthetic judgment, as to the fear that he would be trapped by his words. He aspired to write out of silence into silence: the before and the after were to remain blank. And the "false hands" may only have been the hands of his friends, like Brod, who wanted to make him an author. The publisher's contract raised, for Kafka, the spectre of the artist's betrayal of his vision.

Kafka appears to have been one with modern poets, who again and again have been faced with the fundamental crisis "whether poetry is still possible at all" (Alleman: 110). Put one way, the crisis owes to the widening gap between the sensibility of the modern artist and his linguistic medium: the poet is stunned by a reality sense to which he cannot give expression in words, the resonances of which were accumulated in another, alien time and place. Where language fails, poetry must cease. And it is into this failure, this overwhelming lack, that Kafka endeavors to speak.

Kafka writes with the firm resolve not to say anything. One looks in vain in his mature work for anything like a literal statement. Yet he narrates with realistic, indeed surrealistic, intensity. On the other hand, he as definitively rejects the figurative statement, the metaphor (Alleman: 111). When he does employ a simile, he calls attention to that fact and dismisses it as an image. With a sternness unequaled in modern literature, he rejects both the literal and the non-literal, and thus empties his work of identifiable statement.

It may well be wondered how a man could produce even the modest volume Kafka did without leaving behind more clues to his meaning. That astonishment goes together, perhaps, with the habit of demanding that clues be inserted, here and there, like coupons on a cereal box, available for immediate redemption. It is this demand that Kafka rejects, and his rejection should be the primary clue. The successive withdrawal of every suggestion, the persistent modification of every hint, leaves the reader face to face, in the end, with the inexplicable. Interpretation of a Kafka text succumbs, finally, to the silence of the unutterable. The consummate artistry of Kafka is nowhere more evident: the critic who is not a quack is constrained to follow Kafka down the torturous path to the ineffable, in spite of all contrary inclinations.

The consternation of critics at being unable to determine the "meaning" of Kafka's novels is well known. It is less widely recognized that the achievement of Kafka as regards his novels and his corpus as a whole, can be read, by the trained eye, in some of the parts.

In an especially lucid essay, Beda Alleman has demonstrated that the basic structure of Kafka's stories is this: "the circumstances and possible explanations of what happens are reduced step by step to a core that can no longer be explained" (113). He illustrates the point by reference to Kafka's treatment of the Prometheus myth. In a short prose text of less than a page, Kafka introduces four legends concerning Prometheus. The first is the traditional myth: Prometheus is chained to a rock in the Caucasus for betraying the secrets of the gods to men, and eagles are sent to feed on his liver, which is perpetually renewed. In the second, under the pain of the torture, Prometheus presses himself deeper and deeper into the rock, until he becomes one with it. In the third, the treachery of Prometheus is forgotten over the course of millenia — by the gods, by the eagles, by Prometheus himself. In the fourth, everyone grows weary of the meaningless affair, including the wound, which closes wearily. Kafka closes with this brief paragraph:

There remained the inexplicable mass of rock. — The legend tried to explain the inexplicable. As it came out of a substratum of truth it had in turn to end in the inexplicable.

(*Parables and Paradoxes*: 83)

The final paragraph comes as close as anything Kafka has written to an explicit statement of his intention.

The same structure can be observed in Kafka's parable, "The Silence of the Sirens." In the first paragraph Kafka restates the Homeric story, but with modifications: Odysseus' defensive measures are simplistic, since the Sirens' song could pierce anything, even his wax, and the resolution of those seduced was stronger than chains or masts. So Odysseus sailed out to take the test "in innocent elation."

This restatement of the myth is immediately qualified. Far more seductive than the Sirens' song is their silence. This qualification then requires a further qualification of Odysseus' "innocence," suggested in the first paragraph.

When Odysseus approached, the Sirens actually did not sing. But Odysseus thought he did not hear the song he thought they were singing, and thus escaped the fatal enchantment of that silence.

Kafka has now reversed the roles of song and silence; he has introduced and then qualified the innocence of Odysseus. In the codicil which forms the conclusion, he retrieves Odysseus' guilelessness and leaves the whole affair clouded in mystery: perhaps Odysseus knew that the Sirens were silent and took the pose of innocence as a ruse. But here, Kafka adds, "the human understanding is beyond its depths." The evasion of Odysseus becomes as inexplicable as the rock into which Prometheus was pressed.

Kafka's parables are evidently not illustrations of truths that can be expressed in other, prosaic or literal language. They are not exemplary stories from which a moral can be extracted by drawing a comparison. His parables are thus not parables in any conventional sense. That this is so is unambiguously exemplified by the short but strident piece entitled, "Leopards in the Temple."

124   The text is here quoted in full.

> Leopards break into the temple and drink to the dregs what is in
> the sacrificial pitchers; this is repeated over and over again;
> finally it can be calculated in advance, and it becomes a part of
> the ceremony.
>
>   (*Parables and Paradoxes*: 93)

This parable does not "mean" in the usual sense; it contains no
ready reference to anything outside itself. Like a piece of junk
sculpture, or an abstract painting, it turns in upon itself and
becomes a metaphor of itself. If the parable does not "refer,". it is
because Kafka has painfully severed all possibilities of
coventional or habituated association. Like Prometheus' rock, it
stands inexplicable; it beckons to weariness, to forgetfulness, to
silence. It turns on a center beyond the rim of present sight. It
invites to mystery: the mystery of the unsaid, of what cannot be
said under present historical circumstances.

II

Kafka subjected himself to the discipline of the silence of a
language without apparent patrimony. The words, the grammar,
the phonological system were common property; but these
familiarities were of no assistance in locating the region of his
tongue. He belonged to no place. Yet dumb recognition of his
alien, uncharted wilderness descended like a dense fog on most
who read his work.

Ludwig Wittgenstein subjected himself to the discipline of a
language whose patrimony was a millstone about the neck.
Wittgnstein sought to divest himself of that patrimony, first, by
intensifying its internal logic, and then by "placing" it in a larger
repertoire of language games. The mystique of his work is weird.
Nothing less will explain the fascination of Anglo-Saxon
philosophy for him. It is curious that empiricists and positivists
should have been taken in by an anarchist's tour through the land
of Cartesian certainties.

It is remarkable, in retrospect, to observe what must have been

in the Austrian air earlier in this century (Steiner: 51; Heller: 9f.).
Wittgenstein and Kafka come out of the same region and time.
Not that they were cast in the same mold. Far from it. That both
were able to write German prose with amazing simplicity and
clarity, however, betrays a remarkable affinity. And both seem to
have been drawn inevitably, though by very different routes, to
the problem of language.

In a short but provocative essay on Wittgenstein, Eric Heller
has endeavored to point up the achievement of Wittgenstein as
regards language. In his early work, *Tractatus Logico-
Philosophicus*, finished in 1918 and published in 1921,
Wittgenstein brought the early phase of philosophical language
analysis to its summit. His achievement in this work was
reductive. Heller sums it up thus:

> Compared to the vast dominions that metaphysical thought
> had claimed in the past for its settlements of truth, there is now
> hardly more than a little province of "significant" speech in a
> vast area of silence.
>
> (15)

One can still make some confident assertions about the world, but
in order to speak "essentially," much must be left unsaid. From
the crumbling domain of metaphysics, Wittgenstein recovered
what he could; the rest — the larger part — he consigned to
silence. It is this side of the *Tractatus* that George Steiner
characterizes as "pervaded by the authority of silence" (123).

Wittgenstein interpreters are not wont to read the *Tractatus* as a
small circle of light bordered by a large darkness. Nevertheless,
Wittgenstein fully participated in the shattering of "the
conceptual mirror in which, for two milleniums or more, the
Western consciousness has grown accustomed to seeing itself"
(Hopper: ix). That the tiny fragments remaining could reflect only
sparse light Wittgenstein was fully aware. He was willing to settle
for less light, provided he could escape the prison of language, the
spell cast by habituated parlance over the perceptive powers of the
mind. In *Philosophical Investigations*, a later and more
circumspect work, Wittgenstein acknowledges the

impregnability of that prison:

> A picture held us captive. And we could not get outside it, for it
> lay in our language and language seemed to repeat it to us
> inexorably.
>
> (§115)

Nevertheless, he continued to struggle with his bonds, under the inspiration of a deep distrust of all traditional categories. He espoused the language of everyday as the raw material of his investigations, but wrote an austere, insightful prose that is more akin to his compatriots, Karl Kraus and Franz Kafka, than to the jargon spoken in the streets of Vienna and London. Eric Heller is quite right: in temperament, in conception of the root issue, Wittgenstein is closer to Nietzsche than to Bertrand Russell (20).

Wittgenstein offers interesting commentary on a phenomenon that was emerging just about the time he died (1951): the theatre of the absurd. Note, for example, these sentences from the *Investigations*:

> Philosophy simply puts everything before us, and neither
> explains nor deduces anything. — Since everything lies open
> to view there is nothing to explain.
>
> Philosophy may in no way interfere with the actual use of
> language; it can in the end only describe it.
>
> (§§126, 124)

In 1948 Eugene Ionesco aspired to learn English. He bought an English-French conversation manual and set to work. As he copied and learned the sentences by heart, he discovered that he was not only learning English but some very important truths, such as the fact that a week has seven days, that the ceiling is up, the floor is down, and similar Cartesian certainties. He was so dumbfounded that he decided to share these startling facts in a play: the manual, you may recall, very quickly turns into a dialogue, which is the essence of the drama.

Ionesco's play was called *The Bald Soprano*. In the opening scene, Mr. and Mrs. Smith are seated in the living room. Mr. Smith is reading the paper.

> Mrs Smith: There, it's nine o'clock. We've drunk the soup, and eaten the fish and chips, and the English salad. The children have drunk English water. We've eaten well this evening. That's because we live in the suburbs of London and because our name is Smith.

A little later, Mrs. Smith introduces the children to Mr. Smith:

> Mrs. Smith: Our little boy wanted to drink some beer; he's going to love getting tiddly. He's like you. At table did you notice how he stared at the bottle? But I poured some water from the jug into his glass. He was thirsty and he drank it. Helen is like me: she's a good manager, thrifty, plays the piano. She never asks to drink English beer. She's like our little daughter who drinks only milk and eats only porridge. It's obvious that she's only two. She's named Peggy. . . .
>
> *(Four Plays:* 9f.)

And so Mrs. Smith continues, while her husband reads the *newspaper*. The conversation manual coming to life before one's eyes, language as it's actually used presented in stark array.

Ionesco subtitled his play: *The Tragedy of Language.* He asks, with tongue in cheek, "How could I have allowed myself to make the slightest change in words expressing in such an edifying manner the ultimate truth?" Then he explains:

> Unfortunately the wise and elementary truths they exchanged, when strung together, had gone mad, the language had become disjointed, the characters distorted; words, now absurd, had been emptied of their content . . . For me, what had happened was a kind of collapse of reality.
>
> *(Notes and Counternotes:* 177ff.)

Is there any kinship between Ionesco's reflection and this aphorism of Wittgenstein?

> The results of philosophy are the uncovering of one or another piece of plain nonsense and of bumps that the understanding has got by running its head up against the limits of language. These bumps make us see the value of the discovery.
>
> *(Philosophical Investigations:* §119)

We cannot be sure, but the similarities are suggestive.

As Ionesco discovered his ability as a dramatist by learning

128   English, so Samuel Beckett acquired the discipline of language that enabled him to write *Waiting for Godot* by learning French. "The is a curious phenomenon," observes Martin Esslin (8). Claude Mauriac, in speaking of Beckett, says anyone "who speaks is carried along by the logic of language and its articulations. Thus the writer who pits himself against the unsayable must use all his cunning so as not to say what the words make him say against his will, but to express instead what by their very nature they are designed to cover up: the uncertain, the contradictory, the unthinkable" (Mauriac: 83; quoted by Esslin: 9). Esslin interprets Beckett's use of French as a device to free himself from the conceptual baggage and overtones he would have brought with him to his plays, had he written in his native tongue (9).

The French of Beckett is as clean of resonances as the German of Kafka. But whereas Kafka narrates with intense realism, as though the fantastic world he inhabits were weighted with solid reality, Beckett forms his dialogues in the weightless swirl of a world in collapse. In Act II of *Godot*, Pozzo, now blind, reappears, staggering along behind Lucky, his menial. In Act I Lucky had danced and recited for their entertainment, but he has now fallen dumb. These marks of marginal temporal development, in a play otherwise virtually devoid of temporal sequence, are themselves noteworthy. In any case, at the sight of Vladimir and Estragon, Lucky stops abruptly, Pozzo stumbles into him, and both fall helpless in the clutter of baggage. Pozzo intermittently calls for help as Vladimir and Estragon rehearse how nice it is to have their boredom relieved. At this point Vladimir remarks:

Vladimir:	Poor Pozzo!
Estragon:	I knew it was him.
Vladimir:	Who?
Estragon:	Godot.
Vladimir:	But it's not Godot.
Estragon:	It's not Godot?
Vladimir:	It's not Godot.
Estragon:	Then who is it?
Vladimir:	It's Pozzo.

Pozzo:	Here! Here! Help me up!
Vladimir:	He can't get up.
Estragon:	Let's go.
Vladimir:	We can't.
Estragon:	Why not?
Vladimir:	We're waiting for Godot.
Estragon:	Ah!

(*Waiting for Godot*: 50)

Beckett's work, like Ionesco's, is heavily seasoned with recognition failure: Estragon should know who Pozzo is, but he can't seem to place him from one moment to the next, and he continues to confuse him with Godot, for whom he and Vladimir are vainly waiting. In *The Bald Soprano*, Mr. and Mrs. Martin play a remarkable scene in which they discover their identities as man and wife, by virtue of a long and torturous process of deduction. When they learn that they sleep in the same bed and are parents of the same two-year-old, blond daughter, with one white and one red eye, they fall into each other's arms in happy recognition!

Recognition failure is coupled with dialogic disorientation, which refers to the inability to keep the trajectory of the conversation in focus. In the first part of the brief exchange cited above, Estragon is preoccupied with Godot. Seconds later he has to be reminded that they are, in fact, waiting for Godot. Such disorientation is a constant feature of Beckett's dialogues, and contributes much to the sense of heavy monotony.

There is a third characteristic of conversation in absurd theatre that might be termed hearing loss. Notice how immune Vladimir and Estragon are to the repeated cries of helpless Pozzo. They seem not to hear him. He lies there before their eyes, he has called several times already, yet scarcely six lines later:

Vladimir:	Perhaps we should help him first.
Estragon:	To do what?
Vladimir:	To get up.
Estragon:	He can't get up?
Vladimir:	He wants to get up.
Estragon:	Then let him get up.

Vladimir:	He can't.
Estragon:	Why not?
Vladimir:	I don't know.

(Waiting for Godot: 50)

Language has ceased to function where words are not only misunderstood but not heard at all, where the before and after of word order, of the spiral of dialogue, is out of gear.

In absurd theatre, recognition failure, dialogic disorientation, hearing loss are only a few of the signs pointing to the dissolution of language and therewith the collapse of a home world. In a context totally alien, one does not have a proper name for anything. Nameless objects float free in a multiverse without gravitational vortices. In such a context, language is occasional.

Following a suggestion advanced in Beckett's early novel, *Murphy*, Niklaus Gessner has proposed the thesis that Beckett's dialogues represent the progressive disintegration of language. According to Gessner, positive assertions are "gradually qualified, weakened, and hedged in with reservations until they are completely taken back. In a meaningless universe, it is always foolhardy to make a positive statement" (Esslin: 43; see Gessner). This technique is scarcely distinguishable in principle from Kafka's. And, just as Kafka's work borders a profound silence, so Beckett's drama strains toward an *Act Without Words*. With Beckett dialogue is already an *Endgame*, on the threshold of utter stillness: words die in the throats of his characters, or are emitted as gibberish. Eventually, writes George Steiner, "The first articulate word spoken will bring down the curtain" (52).

The urge to exchange speech for silence, to fall dumb rather than participate in the ossification of parlance, finds its sole counterweight in the commission to witness, in and through speech, to the dissolution of language. It is problematic whether this counterweight is dispensable. The relative failure of Beckett's *Act Without Words I and II* prompts Ihab Hassan to wonder: "Does not this confirm us in the feeling that language is indeed best suited to undermine language, that language expresses the fullness of silence best?" (192f.). Can silence be eloquent wordlessly?

It is not the same thing to fall dumb as to reject the power of language. Literal, unbounded silence is a way of quitting the arena. One may, of course, be driven to quit in the darkness of insanity like Hölderlin and Nietzsche, as the only compromise humanly possible with a world gone askew. But Hölderlin and Nietzsche were born out of season. Metaphorical, qualified silence is the requisite testimony to the powerlessness of language, to its tragic collapse.

Kafka and Wittgenstein, Ionesco and Beckett write in the presence of absence, out of a great lack. They are thus the near kinsmen of Hölderlin and Nietzsche, latter day victims of the death of God, the demise of the divine Word. The oracle of Apollo has fallen mute, beyond earshot of poetic entreaty. Nevertheless, the poet cries out, in the silence of the void. That silence is the horizon of his cry.

III

The effort has been made, in the preceding pair of sketches, to suggest why the Sirens' silence fascinates, why voicelessness may follow modernity. Beyond the horizon lie the shores of silence. Those washed up on such desolate beaches may wish to learn to speak again. Even in the vale of that immense quiet, the being that man is may prompt him to seek a new voice, a new syntax, beholden only to the stillness in which it was conceived.

On the shores of silence what would speech be like? When the crass, harsh cacophonies of dissolute language have died away, what voice might one hope to discover to himself? What grammar would be appropriate to it? What disposition to speech will it be necessary to sustain?

To such questions no certain answer can be given. Yet there is a curious urge to speculate, to reflect out into the void beyond the noise of the world. Speculation of this order need not be academic; it may be practical and productive for living speech in the present. However that may be, overpowering need prompts the effort, on the chance that one may strike a new path in the wilderness of disarray.

Before entertaining a triad of timely linguistic inversions, it may be helpful to mark the way more clearly by taking a detour via the imagination.

In his book, *Christ and Apollo*, William Lynch insists that the only effective path to the goal of the human imagination leads by way of the finite concrete (99f.). To reach its goal, however defined, the imagination must seek straight and unbending entry, despite floods of distortion, into the really real; it must be fully committed to the finite, the concrete, the particular, and yet it must not permit itself to be enslaved or encapsulated by it (*Christ and Apollo*: 40).

The vigor of his insistence on this point is correlative with what he takes to have been the destiny of the imagination in the modern period. According to Lynch, the imagination in our tradition has become a way of circumventing the particular rather than a means of encountering it. The actors on the human stage seem bent on twisting reality in the name of some private dream or infinite; a neurotic civilization tends to construct magical, unreal, or phony mansions in which the soul may dwell (40, 100). Lynch therefore urges a single-minded imaginative pledge to the dense and the definite.

It comes as no surprise, surely, that an analogous constellation of issues comes into view when imagination rather than language is the rubric. Indeed, Ray Hart has written a book on language under the heading of imagination (*Unfinished Man and the Imagination*). He has explored the link between imagination and language in a variety of modes which cannot be pursued explicitly here.

Attention may be called, however, to a striking movement in the authentic imagination, as Lynch depicts it. That movement can be described, tentatively, as the inversion of the obvious. And it is this movement that is to be tracked by way of preparation for inversions of the linguistic order.

The imagination has itself become a vehicle for escaping the finite concrete. Rather than attending the definite, it bounds over the finite in pursuit of some elusive fantasy. The imagination has thus fallen prey to its own failure. It is confined in the prison of its own illusions.

As a corollary, the finite which the imagination thinks it has in view cannot be the real finite; that finite must be a distortion. The imagination thus springs into air from the surface of reality, from a semblance of things.

This line of reasoning permits one to say — and here the inversion appears — that what is taken to be real is illusory; as a consequence, some form of illusion must be the really real. As Northrup Frye has put it:

> Illusion is whatever is fixed or definable, and reality is best
> understood as its negation: whatever reality is, it's not *that*.
>
> (169f.)

Illusion can be defined as the Here, as the fixed and definable, because the literalminded imagination endemic to our age has generated a granite fabric of impenetrable illusion. Henry Miller complains: "My eyes are useless, for they render back only the image of the known" (*Tropic of Capricorn*: 123). So then, the really real is to be located somewhere among those things that pass for illusion in the everyday world.

One need not ponder that inversion long to understand why the transformation of the artist's sensibility (read: the transformation of what he takes to be real) leads him steadily down the road to the Cuckoo's nest: either he or the world must be mad.

If an inversion has taken place, how does the poet or artist become aware of that fact? How does he discover that the senses are being tricked? The answer must be framed carefully.

Out there before him stands the immensely concrete world. It beckons him to attend. But the imagination, because it is attuned to surface dimensions, cannot heed the call. Nevertheless, the imagination, marvelous power that it is, can also *imagine* that it has been duped. Indeed, the lively imagintion perpetually imagines its own disguises, in order not to be easily taken in. We could therefore say that such sensitivity as the imagination initially has, in the face of the inversion, is prompted by some premonition of the disjunction between what it takes to be real and the real really. The first, tentative step is premonition.

The premonition of the disjunction may precipitate a quest for the really real, over against the allegedly real. The quest begins, as we have said, by the imagination calling itself into question; then it calls its sensible objects into question. More accurately: it calls itself and its sensible objects into question at once. The threshold is the presentiment of deception.

Pre-monition and pre-sentiment (the pre- is hyphenated to indicate that one is still in the forecourt) turn away from the self-evident to a tiny fragment — any fragment — of dense, definite reality, like a button discovered in the gutter or the marble staircase in an old vaudeville house (Henry Miller), in an effort to gain a new aperture onto the real. Once discovered, the imagination clings to its fragment for dear life.

A tenuous grasp of some fragment of the immensely concrete may be parlayed, by patience and coaxing, into a new vision of the real. Such new visions are rarely achieved. But where such a momentous event takes place — over a period of time and at the hands of a battery of poets — the imagination is trained on a new "world" that stands in contradiction to the old "world," out of which the new vision arose. The new world becomes the real and the old world the illusory. Of course, from the point of view of those who have not yet made the transition from old to new, the new world appears as a fantasy, as a grand delusion, and its percipient as comic or insane, in short, as poetic. But the transition is customarily so gradual that the common man scarcely knows it has taken place. Only the poets, the harbingers of change, suffer the storms of upheaval.

The imaginative inversion, just described, is suggestive of various aspects of what might be termed the linguistic inversion. Such an inversion in the linguistic sphere, if it is to be timely, must relate in some fundamental way to the dissolution of language and

the temptation to silence. Connections cannot everywhere be
made explicit. Rather, three pairs of terms, the inversion of which
seems appropriate to the present condition of language, are
offered by way of illustration.

1. The first pair may be termed the active/passive inversion.

An active disposition to language, and thus to any contest over
what constitutes reality, leads one to seek to control language, to
domesticate it, to bring it into submission to an already posited
vision of what is there. Analytic philosophy is prompted by an
active disposition to language to free language of its ambiguities,
to make language correspond, insofar as possible, to the clear and
distinct idea, and thus, it assumes, to the real. In the everyday
world, an active relation to speech permits speech to traffic
exclusively in what everybody already knows. Because an active
disposition to language favors the self-evident, it allows only
literal speech: what is there and what is said about what is there
sustain a one-to-one relation to each other.

A passive disposition to language, and thus to any contest over
what constitutes reality, prompts one to seek to release language,
to free it from the tyranny of the self-evident, to allow it to press its
own claims. A passive relation to language is permissive of
ambiguous statement, of the suggestion that the misunderstood or
the not understood hovers by. Because a passive disposition to
language is suspicious of the self-evident, it allows
metaphor: what is said about what is there should never be
collapsed into what is there, for fear of an idolatry of the
appearances. The poet takes up his pen, blurs the foreground of
sight, and waits for the word to strike like lightening.

An active relation to language turns the subject-speaker of the
sentence into a god: the subject-speaker seeks to preside over the
future by virtue of his power to control language.

Listening, hearkening, and keeping silent are the primordial
foundation of a passive relation to language. Only he who is able
to keep silent has something to say.

In the time of the dissolution of language, active and passive are inverted. Active denotes what is in fact a passive relation to language: the active disposition is *acted upon* by what is already in the linguistic tradition and is tyrannized by it. The active disposition can say only what has already been said. The active disposition becomes subject to the fate of a language in which everything is already understood. That fate is to fall dumb.

Passive, on the other hand, denotes what is in fact an active relation to language. The passive disposition holds itself open to the future by standing into the possibilities echoing from repressed language. The passive disposition allows something new to be said. The passive disposition falls silent, hearkens, in order to elude the collapse of degenerate language.

Care for language, like the imaginative quest for the real, involves an initial inversion of the active/passive dichotomy.

2. The second pair may be called the oral/written inversion.

On any reckoning, oral speech is free, untrammeled speech and thus eventful (Ernst Fuchs). Written speech is bound speech: it is transmission of tradition. Under the terms of the inversion here being suggested, oral speech becomes bound and written free. In what respect is that the case?

As free and untrammeled, oral speech brings to expression what has already put in an appearance, what is taken to be real. It reflects what has appeared, but is unreflective in respect of what is to appear.

Written speech, conversely, resists reflecting what has already put in an appearance, but seeks to reflect what is to appear. In sum, written speech is care for language because it is care for being.

The priority of oral over written speech in relation to the question of foundational language is undisputed, but oral speech can only be written in times when the conflict over the real is a root conflict.

Oral and written, in these contexts, are to be understood non-literally. Written speech means to restrain words, language in their power to bring the future under the tyranny of the past.

Restrain means to check the quantity in order to charge the minimal. One writes more in order to speak less; one writes less in order to say more. The poem is restrained speech at its best.

The oral/written inversion transpires in order that oral speech might once again be oral, i.e. eventful.

3. The final form of the inversion does not involve a pair but an agenda. It may be called the grammatical inversion.

In the grammatical tradition of the West stemming from the Greeks and Romans, the fundamental grammatical structure is taken to be the sentence, and the sentence understood as an assertion, with a discrete subject, a verb in the active voice and the indicative mood, and a predicate. The predicate, of course, may take a variety of forms, among which the more common would be a direct object corresponding to a transitive verb, or an adverbial corresponding to an intransitive verb. Another common type is the subjective complement going with a linking verb.

The full and explicit sentence is context-free. Context-free is, to be sure, a relative term. The sentence:

(1) The dog chased the cat.

implies that the speaker has a particular dog and a particular cat in mind. In its present form it falls short of specifying which dog and which cat. We may move in the direction of explicitness by modifying it to read:

(2) The brown and white collie chased the sealpoint Siamese cat.

Even in this form, the sentence is far from fully explicit. One does not yet know which sealpoint Siamese cat, since there must be millions of them extant. Moreover, it is not known where the incident took place, or when. By way of illustration, the sentence may be amplified once more:

(3) The brown and white collie, belonging to Mr. W. R. Smith on Martha's Court, chased the sealpoint Siamese cat, belonging to Mrs. H. E. Pendergast, a neighbor, up Mr. Smith's apple tree on Wednesday, 25 February 1970.

In this expanded form, the sentence wants little by way of further

138 specification. It may now be said to be virtually context-free. The original sentence,

(1) The dog chased the cat.

may also be made context-free by universalizing the assertion. To achieve generalization one could modify the statement to read:

(4) Dogs chase cats.

In either case, explicitness makes it quite possible to utter the statement without surrounding linguistic context, without loss of meaning.

To return now to the initial point, the fundamental grammatical structure which lies at the base of a traditional grammar is the sentence. Since the sentence is conceived as the fundamental unit of language, from which all other aspects of grammar are derived, one must conclude that the sentence is to be understood as the full and explicit sentence, the context-free sentence.

The new science of linguistics, which is another sphere in which language has emerged as a persistent and perplexing problem, has steadfastly refused to accredit traditional grammar. Yet in its early stages, linguistics adopted the dogma of the sentence. At the same time, it insisted on taking its clues from language as it was actually used, much like analytic philosophy. If one asks of particular samples of a language, say English, whether the sentence appears to be the basic grammatical structure, the answer seems to be affirmative. However, linguists were bothered by the definition of the sentence. How do we know, they inquired, where one sentence ends and another begins? In a written text, the period and the capital letter provide unmistakable signals. Punctuation is of course a grammarian's device for interpreting a text, so linguists insisted on using native informants to supply their material. In the case of oral speech the problem was not so simple.

C. C. Fries hit upon a remarkable solution. Rather than starting from a connected prose text, he chose to record *conversations*, in which the beginning and end of periods were marked by changes in speaker. In this way he could say with certainty what group of words constituted a period or a sentence. He produced one of the first ground-breaking studies of the structure of English on the basis of this material.

Two startling features of language emerge as a result of his work. One is the fact that the full, explicit or context-free sentence rarely occurs in language as it is actually used, particularly in its oral form. The context-free sentence thus appears to be a marginal form of the sentence (Ch. III: 29-53) /1/. The second notable result is the fact that many of the periods marked by changes in speakers could not be construed as sentences at all. At best they were sentence fragments, in which something had to be supplied (15ff.) /2/.

To have to supply something to make a group of words subject to grammatical analysis is embarrassing to linguists for two reasons. In the first place, they insist that their discipline is an exact science and deals only with the facts of the case. They are therefore committed to the raw data as they stand. In the second place, some so-called sentence fragments cannot be construed grammatically at all, even by supplying a great deal. To say that they cannot be construed at all, means, of course, that they cannot be construed within the limits of sentence structure. The most recalcitrant of these fragmentary words and word groups consist of what Fries designated "calls" and "attention signals."

The way grammarians and linguists treat greetings, calls, and attention signals is curious. Under the tutelage of the old school grammar, one put them up in the corner when parsing sentences, drew a light line under them, and consigned them to oblivion, grammatically speaking. The new, exact science of linguistics does not appear to have fared any better. In Fries' analysis, "calls" drop out of sight altogether after being once noticed /3/, although he does subsequently isolate a group of words called "attention-getting signals" (his group M[103]). The greeting, "hello," he does not even record in his examples (37, n. 13).

Nevertheless, Fries does note a singular fact about calls, attention-getters, and the like: the majority of them are employed to get a conversation underway, or to renew one when it lags. One picks up the phone and says, "hello," or when one meets a friend on the walk, he begins by saying, "Henry, ..." Then the conversation get underway. Calls thus belong to what Fries terms "situation utterance units": words and word groups that define the context of a conversation (42ff.) /4/.

The model of the conversation provides the essential clue to the grammatical inversion. The call, greeting, attention-getter stand at the threshold of speech, enabling the conversation to get underway. They define the situation in which speech is possible. They do not belong to the sentence, cannot be construed with the sentence, but are the presupposition of the sentence.

Fries himself recognizes the crucial distinction between language-initiating speech and speech as context-bound: "The failure to make this division between 'situation utterance units' and 'response utterance units' seems to me to account for much of the difficulty grammarians have had in making satisfactory statements concerning English sentences" (41, n. 16). He does not, regretfully, develop this important insight.

Beyond the initiating function of the call, the model of the conversation provides one other arresting clue. Fries decided, it will be recalled, to define the utterance unit initially as that unit of speech marked off by changes in speaker. He chose to define this line of demarcation strictly as units bounded by silence on the part of the speaker (to allow for interruptions, etc., that did not impede the flow of speech) (21, 23). As with the sentence, so with the conversation: the greeting, the call, the attention-getter, as situation utterance units, are preceded by silence (37). And Fries includes expressions of leave-taking among the greetings (42, n. 20). The minimum free utterance and the conversation are both bounded, although in different ways, by silence.

A grammar conceived in proximity to needful silence will reverse the priorities of traditional grammar. It will dethrone the sentence and restore to living language its primordial boundary on the edge of the inarticulate. But the poet has no need for the grammarian to teach him that:

So here I am, . . .
. . .
Trying to learn to use words, and every attempt
Is a wholly new start, and a different kind of failure
Because one has only learnt to get the better of words
For the thing one no longer has to say, or the way in which
One is no longer disposed to say it. And so each venture
Is a new beginning, a raid on the inarticulate
. . .

(Eliot: 16)

There, on the edge, language takes its rise.

In a grammar concocted on the shores of silence, the fundamental, underived structure of language is taken to be the vocative. The vocative can be understood either as naming or as calling.

The vocative as call is both active and passive: it is calling and being called, in one integral movement. Calling presupposes a call, but it is also a hearkening to a call that has not yet become audible. At the same time, calling can only be a response to a call: man speaks because he is first spoken to.

The plaintive lament of voiceless man in a noisy world is an entreaty to be called. The initial stammering of the poet is a tentative hearkening to a faint and distant tolling, a plea in the service of the inner ear. The outburst of the prophet is a cry to be spared the exactions of the divine word.

The vocative also names. It is the destiny of the being that has language to name, and to be named. Man names in order to place. Naming brings a world to stand out of the chaos of silence. But the namer is also named. The being of man is being-with: The community to which man belongs is a mutual naming. Adam names and is named, by the gods, by his fellows, by the birds of the air and the beasts of the field; even the rocks cry out the name of man.

The grammatical structure most closely related to the vocative is the imperative. The imperative is the call coming to expression as truncated sentence. In the imperative sentence

(5) Listen!

the real "subject" of the sentence, the one commanding, is

142 grammatically hidden: it does not find expression in the structure of the sentence at all. The grammatical subject of the sentence, the one commanded, is either suppressed, as in the preceding example, or it is expressed as the vocative:

(6) John, listen!

(7) Listen, you!

The call breaks into language first as a vocative, and then as a sentence fragment in the form of the imperative. The imperative can be understood either as a calling or a being called: one both gives and receives commands.

The basic form of the sentence is the passive. In the passive sentence, such as

(8) I was told to listen

the "subject," by which is meant the performer of the action, is suppressed as a means of attending the call. The example does not say by whom I was told, though the "by whom" may be added to the passive sentence, as a means of making the sentence more explicit:

(9) I was told to listen by my muse.

In its less explicit form, the passive is the imperative raised intitially to full sentence form. For the first time both a discrete subject and a discrete predicate are given full grammatical status. However, the subject of the sentence is not yet the performer of the action; the subject remains the recipient.

As language moves in the direction of explicitness, into the realm of the context-free utterance, it leaves less and less to the context of con-versation out of which it arose. The call is stopped down or forgotten. At that juncture, the speaker of the sentence asserts himself. Either he becomes the performer of the action and thus the grammatical subject of the sentence, or he nominates the subject of the sentence and determines the predicates that apply. As language approaches full specificity, as it attains the complexity necessary for the development of a high culture, the grammarian finds it more and more difficult to bring the phenomena under sharp control. The highly developed languages, such as Greek or Latin, or one of the modern literary languages, is a very complicated affair.

Nevertheless, two final suggestions regarding the grammatical inversion may be risked. Both have to do with the phenomenon called mood.

The subjunctive mood, the distinctive form of which has now virtually disappeared from English, is the mood of probability or possibility. We may say,

(10) Aunt Nan may come tomorrow

or

(11) If spring were only here, . . .

and mean by the mood that we are entertaining a possible state of affairs, about which a more definite statement would not be appropriate. The indefiniteness of the mood prompts this definition: the subjunctive sentence is an assertion in a temporal horizon.

Lack of definiteness, and absence of bold precision, places the subjunctive assertion in the flux of time. The erosive hands of time make a mockery of certainties. The subjunctive is thus care for time.

It follows that the indicative sentence is an assertion in an atemporal horizon. With the indicative language arrives at the possibility of full specificity. The way we say and thus what we say may be lifted out of the temporal succession and redeemed from the encroachments of history. That is no mean achievement. Discursive thinking rests on the approximation of a context-free language, of an arbitrarily deployable set of verbal counters. With this development, man enters upon his visible history.

At the same time, a fully explicit, context-free language also makes it possible for man, the maker and user of language, to turn away from the phenomena and circle in the orbit of his own thought. The sentence assertion is the most derived form of language. As a maker of sentences, he can readily forget the well of silence from which language is drawn. He can grow deaf to the call. He then comes to live in proximity but not in relation to things. His language makes him a prisoner in a cell without windows or door.

The grammatical inversion is a total reversal of traditional grammatical priorities, in the interests of man's openness to the wonder of being.

/1/ Fries classifies all his materials in one or the other of two categories: (1) utterance units which *begin* conversations; (2) utterance units which occur as *responses* to other utterance units (37). In principle, then, no unit of his material could be said to be context-free.

/2/ Although Fries takes note of this phenomenon, especially in chastizing traditional grammarians, he proceeds to ignore it in his own analysis of the materials.

/3/ Calls are referred to pp. 44, 51, 53, but are ignored in the grammatical analysis.

/4/ Fries notes that greetings and calls together constitute only 5% of his material (51). This is one reason grammarians ignore them. The more significant reason for shunting them aside, however, is that they cannot be construed grammatically. The small incidence of calls owes, of course, to their limited function in relation to the body of speech. As linguistics moves more in the direction of sentence transcending analysis, calls will no doubt rise to greater prominence, particularly if the analysis is strictly empirical.

EPILOGUE

I waited impatiently for the light to change. A truck rumbled by, its erect phallus belching smoke, the briefcase in my hand grew suddenly leaden, a student cyclist spat at my feet as he rode past. Finally I stepped from the curb. As I fell, I remember hearing the chancellor intone, ". . . and all the rights and privileges thereto appertaining . . .."

Epilogue

People, especially scholars, are rarely given to the luxury of an unhurried conversation of the type in which one listens. We talk to each other a great deal, but we do not hear what is said in return. Indeed, we do not pay attention to what we ourselves say. It is as though conversants were mouths without ears. And we tend to write in the same mode: a paragraph or an essay is an occasion to manhandle the subject and browbeat readers.

Because the author is or ought to be the preeminent reader of any work, I have endeavored to compose the preceding essays as though I were reading them. I have tried not to mouth words for their flavor and I have sought to avoid being preoccupied with thoughts. This is another way of saying that I have attempted to pay attention to the phenomena being described and analyzed, to let the subject matter speak for itself.

The reader is invited to follow suit. If significant subject matter is being addressed, the author should not be permitted to interfere with the presentation. The reader should attune the ear to such echoes of the theme as may linger in the words.

149

I

The essays which comprise this book were composed, in their original forms, over a period of time. They were not designed to go in a single, coherent book. Yet, in retrospect, this group of papers appeared to form a suggestive configuration. A few reflections on the shape of the whole may be of assistance to the reader.

Part I, "Jesus as Precursor," is related to Part II, "Voices of Silence," as speech is to silence. In the analysis of forms of discourse, attention is usually devoted to what is *said*. But if clues dropped by writers like Kafka, Beckett, Wittgenstein, and even Miller are heeded, silence is an essential ingredient in authentic speech. One should therefore deliberately attend to what is *not* said, at the same time one is listening to what is said.

An analysis of silence presents a major methodological problem. How does one go about dissecting the *unsaid*? As a first modest step, perhaps it is sufficient to call attention to the need. "Siren's Song Without Sound" suggests what a syntax conceived in silence may be like.

In each of the essays in Part I, the attempt has been made to juxtapose Jesus and a more recent figure. The juxtaposition occurs differently in the various essays, and no doubt with varying success.

The treatment of Jesus in "Jesus and Kafka" goes together with the theme *precursor* as sketched by Borges. Indeed, the essays in this whole group are informed by this fundamental insight. In "Jesus and Kafka" nothing more could be said of Jesus without spoiling the theme. In the four essays, or pairs of essays, which follow, the notion of hidden precursor is progressively betrayed: Jesus figures evermore explicitly.

The studies of *Waiting for Godot* and the Parable of the Mustard Seed are set side by side because the latter appeared to be thematic in the former: the inept tree. Two literary forms so divergent can scarcely be compared. Yet, the two invite comparison, on the grounds that one may be understood as precursor of the other. The relationship of the one to the other is developed in the appendix, "In Place of Questions." An author often puts questions at the end of a chapter, particularly in a textbook, to assist the reader in recalling the major points just enumerated. Since questions seemed inappropriate in essays without "points," triads of theses were substituted. This appendix constitutes a theological treatise in nuce.

Similarly, the studies of Miller and Castaneda called for alignment with the methodological study of the parable of the Leaven. The affinities between these two essays become apparent only in retrospect. Once again, it is not plausible to compare Henry Miller and Carlos Castaneda with Jesus. But in some important respects Jesus appears to be a precursor of the two.

In the essays on "Jesus as Magician" and "Jesus as Saunterer," Jesus is more explicitly brought into juxtaposition with Maurice Conchis in Fowles' novel, *The Magus*, and Henry David Thoreau. Yet even here the connections are metaphorical. Jesus is not a magician in the same sense as Maurice Conchis. But the function of Conchis — Nicolas Urfe reflects, on the basis of his first encounter with Conchis, "something was trying to slip between me and reality" (116) — illuminates the function of Jesus, — or is it the other way around? Further, silence is thematic in Fowles' story: "there are times when silence is a poem" (521). And, it is surprising that the similarities of Thoreau as walker and Jesus as stroller have not struck the critic before now.

II

It would be too much to claim that these essays endeavor to interpret Jesus and Kafka, Jesus and Beckett, etc. To interpret is to say what something or someone means. This work does not aspire to so much. The task of description, though a less exciting enterprise, is no less rewarding. In some ways it is an even more difficult task. To see what is really there in a text, one is inclined to stare, unblinking. But when one is on the lookout for precursors,

152   the subject matter will tolerate no more than a glimpse. Precursors are fleeting. Don Juan recommends the "smoke" in order to give the eyes the speed they need. And one must be circumspect: close attention should be coupled with the indifferent glance.

The implications of these descriptions have not been drawn out in fully explicit language. There is probably far too much explicitness as it is. Pure descriptions should permit the reader to draw his or her own conclusions, which may not be the same ones the author would and does draw, but which would not necessarily, for that reason, be wrong. In so far as the descriptions intimidate the reader, they fail of their purpose.

These descriptions aspire, furthermore, to be appropriate to the subject matter they are attempting to portray. To describe Jesus is to let him speak for himself, so to speak. But he cannot easily do so from out of and under a long tradition of interpretation which may have muffled his voice. Hence, it seems necessary to let Jesus' real successors discover him to us. In so doing, Jesus is also identified as precursor. In this quest description and juxtaposition are the correlative techniques.

III

These essays have a context of which the readers should not, perhaps, be unaware. Context here refers to what is being held in view simultaneously though wordlessly. However, if silence is broken on the subject of context, it should be done so in a mode correlative with the rest of the work. In this case, only description and juxtaposition are permitted. The description itself should be laconic in the interests of restrained speech.

At the time the earliest of the preceding essays was drafted, the subject matter clamoring for and getting attention was the state of contemporary theology, specifically Christian theology. I was teaching at the time in a seminary. The prospects of theology and its learning and teaching were of daily concern and conversation. About that time I wrote something like the following.

Theologians would be blinking all barometers if they did not admit that the immediate prospects of theology are grim indeed. The foundations of theology have been steadily eroded by virtue of the fact that there is little or nothing in the arena of modern human experience to which theology can appeal in articulating the claim of the ancient faith. In desperation theology seems to have gone awhoring after the scientific fleshpots of Egypt. One appears to be left with the choice, consequently, of retiring to the monastic ghetto and perpetuating, in cloistered precincts, the now archaic tongue of the Christianized age, or of abandoning the tradition altogether in favor of a secular surrogate.

The choice thus posed did not and does not greatly appeal to me. It may be conceded that theology has wandered so far afield as to have forgotten the wellsprings of its infancy. In this respect one may prefer secularity to the perpetuation of a defunct tradition, which is only saying that one prefers nothing to an idle exercise. Nevertheless, if the history of theology is any index to its potential cultural significance, it would appear to be ill advised to abandon any locus where the human question might possibly be prosecuted. For the question facing theology just now is not merely the fate of the Christian faith, but the fate of man.

If theology is to address the human question, the study of theology ought to begin these days with a study of poetry, that is, of poiesis in the root sense. For example, the study of Nietzsche, Kafka, Borges, Camus, Miller, Beckett, Ionesco and the like, may be sufficiently strong medicine to induce theology, once the queen of the humanities, to shake off her torpor. At all events, theology is uniquely prepared, by virtue of her history, to participate in preparing the way for the creation, recognition, and reception of liberating poiesis, if and when it comes.

Poiesis is liberating when it dispels illusion, or so these essays have endeavored to claim. The poetic destination is Away-from-here because the disjunction of the times and the intensification of illusion have conspired to cloak the real. When the eye betrays vision, when the ear impairs hearing, when ideas suffocate the mind, the poet sets out for Away-from-here: that is his destination because the real is his goal.

154   Theology, like poetry, has a history of altering the face of the world, of reality. Under the aegis of the Christian faith the ancient pagan demons and powers were swept from the skies, thus paving the way for the scientific conquest of nature. It was the impact of theology, directly and indirectly, that produced the modern historical consciousness — the notion that man is responsible for his own destiny and the destiny of the world — and with it the relativizing of every point of view, including theology's own. It is not too much to expect of theology that it join in the quest for the real in our time, even if that means emancipating itself from every apologetic ploy on behalf of the Christian faith. The theological question, i.e. the god question, is no longer central for theology; christology survives primarily as a human question. The real *theological* issue is whether man can find a concrete context for his existence, a real world to which he can give himself. And it is this *human* question to which theology is increasingly devoting itself.

Realism dictates, however, that hope remain marginal. Both poetry and theology have suffered anemia. Avant-garde poetry is prone to hanker after a pre-logical, pre-modern mytho-poetic consciousness, which it believes alone can offset the devastating effects of scientism. Primitivism in poetry seeks to blink the secular landscape of the modern world. Radical theology, on the other hand, is the progeny, by and large, of Karl Barth, so that it tends to yearn for an apocalyptic correction of history. Apocalypticism shirks human responsibility for history. In spite of these reservations, there are promising omens: young theologians have abandoned the priesthood wholesale to become artists and poets, even sorcerers. The one place where the human question is likely to gain a hearing today is where theologians are talking to artists, poets, and those who wish to speak a word for NATURE. There is evidence, slender though it is, that a new poetic tradition is taking root. It has spilled over into the theatre, the nightclub, the public park, and here and there even into the classroom. The rejuvenation of poetry and the transformation of theology cannot be far behind when it perceived that man's destiny hangs in the balance.

Optimism must be tempered with the enormity of the task set before poets and theologians. Since theology is the context of these essays, certain suggestions concerning the shape of theology's part of the task have emerged as a byproduct of these studies. As may be anticipated, the root issue is the relation of the Christian faith to reality. Around this issue turn numerous other questions, theoretical and practical. The suggestions which follow are divided into three groups: those which concern theology itself; those which have to do with the milieu in which theology is undertaken; and those which touch upon the learning and teaching of theology, since the academic institution seems to be the place where theology is most often prosecuted.

1. Theology itself

1.1 Theology must become preoccupied with our fundamental history, with the history of the Western tradition as it empties out into and shapes the present, including the historical litter that comes with the Christian tradition.

   The most significant form of this preoccupation is the play between the shape of the tradition in various periods of the past and the shape of the present situation. This is a call for the deepening of historical criticism.

1.2 Theology must give rapt attention to the way modern man experiences reality, not, of course, to the way he thinks he experiences it, but to the "worlds" which form the horizons of his existence.

   For this reason, theology will have to work in close conjunction with arts and letters, with certain movements in the classical disciplines, and with the raw data of existence that is pressed up against its limits.

1.3 Theology must take on the task of reassessing what is given to it: such a reassessment will emerge from the interplay between interpretation of tradition and experience of reality.

1.4 Theology will have to indulge in the deformation of the language tradition if it hopes to achieve its purpose.

1.5 Theology will be future oriented in the sense that it will ferret out the trajectory of our fundamental history and extrapolate from it the "upon which" of its constructive work. It will have the courage to take the risk of that construction upon itself.

1.6 Theology must be raised from a conglomerate of externally related disciplines to a discipline with its own integrity and rationale.

It will not, therefore, be oriented to any other discipline as such.

1.7 Theology should sail into the contest over reality or strike its colors.

2. The context of theology

2.1 Theology should forsake the cloistered precincts of the church, where nothing real is being addressed, in favor of a radical openness to mundane experience.

It is quite possible that authentic theology in the future will be prosecuted in the secular university and/or in the parish church, especially the disestablished type.

2.2 Theology should quit the shelter of ecclesiastical traditions in the interest of a non-apologetic assessment of those traditions, with reference to the way in which they touch and are touched by reality.

2.3 Theology should desist in its practice of raping the intellect, affections and will of man, for its own apologetic pleasure, in the interest of its own and man's manhood.

2.4 The conflict between theology and the church should be abandoned from the side of theology: the conflict indicates that theology wishes to establish itself as the fountainhead of *Gemeindetheologie* (church theology).

2.5 The split between academic theology and professional training requires resolution, but not in favor of one or the other: the resolution must look to the learning and practice of theology in proximity to the raw indifference, antipathy, and even sympathy of the secular world.

2.6   The divisions among the historical, systematic (contemporary), and practical disciplines should be resolutely exorcized; the divisions do not represent a division of labor or the hermeneutical circle, but three competing bases for theology, no one of which is any longer viable:

The basis of the historical disciplines, which are clandestinely grounded in the authority of the Bible and tradition, has completely eroded;

The basis of the systematic disciplines, which are openly grounded in the authority of the clear and distinct idea and thus in the Enlightenment, and in the cogency of the self-enclosed system and thus in the 19th century, has been shattered beyond repair;

The basis of the practical disciplines, which are patronizingly grounded in the needs of the churches, has become illegitimate because the needs of the church are no longer an index to anything significant.

2.7   Every institution harboring the practice of theology should have cold beer on tap in its common room.

3.   The learning and teaching of theology

3.1   The learning and teaching of theology require a new form of monasticism, in which intense, rigorous preoccupation with irrelevant things, such as a button discovered in the gutter, takes place in uncloistered precincts.

3.2   The learning and teaching of theology needs to be freed from the fetters of conventional pedagogy, since conventional pedagogy retards the maturation of both student and teacher and thus inhibits the deepening of the subject matter of theology:

The lecture method should be abandoned as the fundamental teaching medium since it is linked, in the American tradition, with the passing on of information; it should be reinstated as the primary medium of passing on the issue of reflective labor to the whole of the proximate theological community, as in the older European tradition.

Teachers and students should learn to read and think, alone and together, with reference to everything from the *New York Times* to the Rosetta Stone.

Writing should be the prerequisite of every uttered word so that one may know whether one is thinking when talking. If the scholar and student wrote more, they would write less, and thus save wear and tear on eye and mind.

The courses structure of the curriculum should be abandoned and a course structure substituted: the student should be apprenticed to a scholar or scholars so that he or she may learn the craft. Students who run out of rope should be given a certificate and sent away; the rest should be kept until their careers have taken discernible shape.

The subject matter base of the curriculum should be formally contracted but substantively expanded.

3.3 Teacher and student should never be more than arm's length from the cream of what has been written (institutional libraries should be distributed to locations where teachers and students spend the bulk of their time).

3.4 The teacher should afford the student the same scholarly freedom he grants himself, and should demand of the student the same standards as he demands of himself: what he does not give to and expect from the student he will soon not give to and expect from himself. The student, like the importunate widow, should worry the teacher until the student has the allegedly self-evident point in his own hands: he will be doing himself and the teacher a favor in so doing.

3.5 Teachers should learn that their first professional responsibility is to theology, their second to their students; they do not have a third that is not included in the other two. Students should learn that their first professional responsibility is to theology, their second is to their teachers; they do not have a third that is not included in the other two.

3.6 The learning and teaching of theology should not be regarded as a thing of and for itself, but of and for the subject matter, what is at issue.

3.7   All teachers and students of theology should learn to fly-fish, wander in the wilderness, and bake bread.

WORKS CONSULTED

Alleman, Beda
1967   "Metaphor and Antimetaphor." Pp. 103-23 in *Interpretation: The Poetry of Meaning*. Edited by S. R. Hopper and David L. Miller. New York: Harcourt, Brace & World.

Beckett, Samuel
1954   *Waiting for Godot. A Tragicomedy in Two Acts*. New York: Grove Press, Inc.

Borges, Jorge Luis
1964a   *Labyrinths. Selected Stories and Other Writings*. Edited by Donald A. Yates and James E. Irby. New York: New Directions Publishing Corporation.

1964b   *Other Inquisitions, 1937-1952*. Translated by Ruth L. C. Simms, with an introduction by James E. Irby. New York: Simon & Schuster.

Bornkamm, Günther
1960   *Jesus of Nazareth*. Translated by Irene and Fraser McLuskey, with James M. Robinson. New York: Harper & Brothers.

Bultmann, Rudolf
1963   *History of the Synoptic Tradition*. Revised edition. Translated by John Marsh. New York: Harper & Row.

Camus, Albert
1969   *The Myth of Sisyphus and Other Essays*. Translated by Justin O'Brien. New York: Alfred A. Knopf.

Castaneda, Carlos
1974   *Tales of Power*. New York: Simon & Schuster.

1972   *Journey to Ixtlan: The Lessons of Don Juan*. New York: Simon & Schuster.

1971   *A Separate Reality: Further Conversations with Don Juan*. New York: Simon & Schuster.

1968   *The Teachings of Don Juan: A Yaqui Way of Knowledge*. New York: Simon & Schuster.

161

162

Dibelius, Martin
1956   *Botschaft und Geschichte.* Volume II. Tübingen: J. C. B. Mohr (Paul Siebeck).

Dodd, C. H.
1961   *The Parables of the Kingdom.* Revised edition. New York: Charles Scribner's Sons.

Eliot, T. S.
1943   *Four Quartets.* New York: Harcourt, Brace.

Esslin, Martin
1961   *The Theatre of the Absurd.* New York: Doubleday & Co., Inc.

Fowles, John
1969   *The French Lieutenant's Woman.* Boston: Little, Brown & Co.

1965   *The Magus.* New York: Dell Publishing Co., Inc.

Fries, C. C.
1952   *The Structure of English: An Introduction to the Structure of English Sentences.* New York: Harcourt, Brace & World.

Frye, Northrup
1967   *Anatomy of Criticism.* New York: Atheneum.

Gessner, Niklaus
1957   *Die Unzulänglichkeit der Sprache.* Zürich: Jaris.

Gospel of Thomas
1959   *The Gospel According to Thomas.* Coptic text established and translated by A. Guillaumont, et al. New York: Harper & Brothers.

Hart, Ray L.
1970   "The American Home-World: Reality and Imagination." Lecture delivered in a series "Imagination and Contemporary Sensibility." University of Montana, inaugurating the Department of Religious Studies.

1968   *Unfinished Man and the Imagination.* New York: Herder & Herder.

WORKS CONSULTED

Hassan, Ihab   163
1967   *The Literature of Silence*. New York: Alfred A. Knopf,
              Inc.

Heller, Eric
1969   "Wittgenstein: Unphilosophical Notes." Pp. 3-24 in *New
              Essays on Religious Language*. Edited by Dallas M. High.
              New York: Oxford University Press.

Hopper, Stanley Romaine
1967   "Introduction." Pp. ix-xxii in *Interpretation: The Poetry
              of Meaning*. Edited by S. R. Hopper and David L. Miller.
              New York: Harcourt, Brace & World.

              Interpreter's Dictionary of the Bible. Volumes III and IV.
              Edited by G. A. Buttrick.

Ionesco, Eugene
1964   *Notes and Counternotes*. Translated by Donald Watson.
              New York: Grove Press, Inc.

1958   *Four Plays*. Translated by Donald M. Allen. New York:
              Grove Press, Inc.

Jeremias, Joachim
1965   *The Parables of Jesus*. Revised edition. Translated by S.
              H. Hooke. New York: Charles Scribner's Sons.

Jülicher, Adolph
1963   *Die Gleichnisreden Jesu*, Zweiter Teil, *Auslegung der
              Gleichnisreden der drei ersten Evangelien*. Darmstadt:
              Wissenschaftliche Buchgesellschaft.

Kafka, Franz
1961   *Parables and Paradoxes*. New York: Schocken Books.

1956   *The Trial*. New York: The Modern Library.

Lohmeyer, Ernst
1958   *Evangelium des Matthäus*, herausgegeben von Werner
              Schmauch. Göttingen: Vandenhoeck & Ruprecht.

Lynch, William
1960   *Christ and Apollo*. New York: Sheed & Ward, Inc.

164

Mauriac, Claude
1958   *L'alittérature contemporaine*. Paris: Albin Michel.

Melville, Herman
1950   *Moby Dick*. New York: Random House, Inc.

Merleau-Ponty, Maurice
1964   *The Primacy of Perception and Other Essays*. Translated and edited by James M. Edie. Evanston: Northwestern University Press.

Miller, Henry
1961   *Tropic of Capricorn*. New York: Grove Press, Inc.

Nietzsche, Friedrich
1954   *The Portable Nietzsche*. Selected and translated by Walter Kaufman. New York: The Viking Press, Inc.

Politzer, Heinz
1966   *Franz Kafka: Parable and Paradox*. Ithaca: Cornell University Press.

Reich, Charles A.
1970   *The Greening of America*. New York: Random House.

Ricoeur, Paul
1967   "New Developments in Phenomenology in France: The Phenomenology of Language." *Social Research* 34: 1-30.

Roszak, Theodore
1969   *The Making of a Counter Culture*. Garden City, New York: Doubleday & Co., Inc.

Schorer, Mark, et al.
1948   *Criticism: The Foundations of Modern Literary Judgment*. Edited by Mark Schorer, et al. New York: Harcourt, Brace & World.

Schweitzer, Albert
1956   *The Mysticism of Paul the Apostle*. Translated by William Montgomery. London: Adam & Charles Black.

Smith, B. T. D.
1937   *The Parables of the Synoptic Gospels: A Critical Study*. Cambridge: At the University Press.

WORKS CONSULTED

Smith, C. W. F.
1948   *The Jesus of the Parables*. Philadelphia: Westminster Press.

Steiner, George
1967   *Language and Silence: Essays on Language, Literature, and the Inhuman*. New York: Atheneum.

Thoreau, Henry David
1950   *Walden and Other Writings*. Edited, with an introduction by Brooks Atkinson. New York: Random House, Inc.

      "Walking." Pp. 597-632 in *Walden and Other Writings*.

Updike, John

1963   *The Centaur*. Greenwich, Connecticut: Fawcett Publications, Inc.

Wilder, Amos M.
1971   *Early Christian Rhetoric. The Language of the Gospel*. Cambridge: Harvard University Press.

Wittgenstein, Ludwig
1963   *Philosophical Investigations*. Translated by G. E. M. Anscombe. Oxford: Basil Blackwell.

1960   *Tractatus Logico-Philosophicus*. Eighth printing. London: Routledge & Kegan Paul, Ltd. (original 1922).

Wolfe, Tom
1969   *The Electric Kool-Aid Acid Test*. New York: Bantam Books, Inc.

SEMEIA SUPPLEMENTS

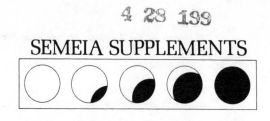

The Sword of His Mouth
Forceful and Imaginative Language in Synoptic Sayings
ROBERT C. TANNEHILL

The Sword of His Mouth is a study of the rhetorical and poetic form of synoptic sayings which argues that many of these sayings use a "depth rhetoric" which seeks to challenge the hearer's fixed structures of meaning and value, moving him to new action by awakening new insight. This study brings to light important but neglected features of the texts and demonstrates the value of this new approach for gaining fresh insight into their significance. Special attention is given to pattern and tension. An attempt is made to show how form and content merge in producing utterances with provocative verbal power.

Jesus emerges from this study as one whose language must be distinguished from casual speech.

The Sword of His Mouth is available for $3.50 to members of sponsoring societies of Scholars Press (order no. 060601 from Scholars Press). Others must pay the full retail price of $4.95 and order from Fortress Press.

Sponsored by the Society of Biblical Literature and
Co-published by Scholars Press and Fortress Press